The
Art
of
Believing
&
Achieving

Jamel Dorsey

---

*LEARN HOW TO MATERIALIZE
YOUR DREAMS*

© 2016 by Jamel Dorsey. All rights reserved.

No part of this book may be reproduced in any written, electronic, recording, or photocopying form without written permission of the author.

Published by: Banks Publishing
Cover Design by: Jamel Dorsey
Editing by: Julie Webb
Photographer: Karissa Dohrman
ISBN: 978-0692769546
1. Self-Help 2. Personal Growth
First Edition

Printed in the United States of America

DEDICATION

To the most loving person I have ever known, my Grandmother Betty A. Ritter. You are truly missed. And to Edward "Speedy" Hicks your presence will always be remembered with love.

CONTACT & BOOKING

 JAMEL DORSEY

 JAMEL DORSEY

CONTENTS

HOW TO READ THIS BOOK............1
YOU EXIST FOR A REASON..............3
FOCUS AND IT WILL COME INTO BEING.......6
DON'T LIMIT YOUR DREAMS............9
FIND A PROBLEM AND SOLVE IT......13
THE ENGINEERING OF GREATNESS......17
CREATE THE LIFE YOU WANT...................21
TURNING YOUR IDEAS INTO A BUSINESS.....25
THE TRUTH ABOUT BUSINESS.................31
VALUE IS IN THE EYE OF THE BEHOLDER.......38
INVENT THE FUTURE.............41
BE CREATIVE...................46
EXPECT PROBLEMS........................48
LEARN..............51
COMMIT TO YOUR PURPOSE.........53
DO WHAT YOU LOVE..............57
IS COLLEGE FOR YOU?...................61
THE ENTREPRENEURIAL MIND..........65
FIND A NEED...........70
WHAT CAN YOU IMPROVE?............75

WHO WANTS TO BE A MILLIONAIRE?..........78
LET SUCCESS INVADE YOUR MIND................81
WHAT DO YOU WANT TO ACCOMPLISH?...84
MAKE PROGRESS UNTIL ACCOMPLISHED......87
BELIEVE IN YOURSELF OR STARVE............90
THE POWER OF PATIENCE....................94
THE POWER OF WORDS............................98
THE POWER OF BELIEF........................103
THE POWER INSIDE YOU........108
DEFEAT SELF-DEFEATING THOUGHTS.......113
FIGHT FOR YOUR DREAMS...........118
P.U.S.H..............122
TAKING FINANCIAL RISKS................124
MONEY MANAGEMENT...........127
INVEST IN YOURSELF........................134
KEEP YOUR CREDIT HEALTHY...........137
BUSINESS PARTNERSHIPS.............141
THE ECONOMY'S PULSE....................147
THE HEART & SOUL OF BUSINESS...........151
PAY OFF YOUR DEBT........154
DIVERSIFYING YOUR PORTFOLIO...........158
THE ART OF SELLING........165

THE ART OF MARKETING.........171
THE ART OF BRANDING..................171
TALENTED POOR PEOPLE........176
WHAT'S HOLDING YOU BACK........180
LAZINESS WILL STEAL YOUR DREAMS........184
YOU OWE THE WORLD.............187
CHANGE YOUR ATTITUDE..........190
LIFE IS PRECIOUS........193
PEACE OVER MONEY...........197
THE ART OF BELIEVING & ACHIEVING......206

> "YOUR PURPOSE IN LIFE IS TO FIND YOUR PURPOSE AND GIVE YOUR WHOLE HEART AND SOUL TO IT"
>
> — GAUTAMA BUDDHA

HOW TO READ THIS BOOK

Your birth was no mistake because mistakes are not made on purpose. Although, your parents may not have planned you, the one who rules the universe did. In fact, everything that has transpired in your life up until this very second, has happened because it's preparing you for a moment that has yet to come. Therefore, I wrote this book with the intent to help you prepare for that moment, by teaching you how to get acquainted with your purpose in life.

So I have written what I like to call, "Daily Reflections," which are designed to help you bring the expanse of what you are into the expression of who you are by helping you discover your unique place in the universe. There are no chapters, only various subject matters which I carefully fix my thoughts upon using my own personal experiences and the experiences of others to empower you and to help you focus on what's best for you. So that you can live a more rewarding, fulfilling and balanced life. For this reason, my goal is to help inspire you to do what you feel you were put here to do. Perhaps you have the qualities of an athlete, have an ear for music, or an eye for fashion. Whatever it may be this book is intended to help you step from out of the shadows and into your light. Because having a gift is one thing, but walking in your purpose while utilizing your gift is another.

Therefore, my hope is that this book will help push you to live closer to the center of your being throughout the duration of your life journey. So by the energy and power that has been invested in me, may this body of knowledge, and wisdom help you become what you aspire to be.

YOU EXIST FOR A REASON

From birth the heart lives out its purpose, and so should you. As the first organ to form as the human body develops. The heart beats anywhere between 60-80 times per minute, 3,600-4,800 times an hour, 86,400-115,200 times a day, and over 30 million times a year. The hearts primary responsibility is to circulate blood throughout the body. So that it can help supply oxygen to the brain and other organs. The heart does this 24 hours a day, 7 days a week, around the clock, non-stop.

So as long as your heart keeps beating you should never want to stop achieving because life is made up of time and our days are measured in hours and once time is lost, it's never found again. Therefore, we should always relate time to movement from here to there takes time. Any distance to be covered, or goal we want to accomplish, requires time.

In Duane Elgin's book, *The Living Universe*, he writes "We are each original and there will never be another person like you in all eternity." In other words, you're unique every characteristic and distinguishing trait you possess is what makes you—you! So when you know what your mission in life is, you become clear on what your mission in life is not.

So why continue to waste another minute drifting through life aimlessly? Because we both know it's time for you to connect with your purpose in order to fulfill your destiny. What are your hopes and dreams for your future? How well are you managing your goals as well as your time? What steps are you taking towards your inner ambitions? And if you haven't started yet then what's stopping you?

The world is full of opportunities you just have to open up your eyes to see them. There are over 28 million small businesses in the United States alone according to the Small Business Administration's Office of

Advocacy. So there's absolutely no reason for you to give up on what you aspire to be.

Furthermore, the universe is one big sea of energy and it carries an abundant supply of resources that are always readily available at our disposal. With this in view, I encourage you to master you, and find your path. The ancient Chinese Philosopher Lao Tzu once said "Knowing others is intelligence; but knowing yourself is true wisdom. Mastering others is strength; but mastering yourself is true power." When you know yourself it also helps you know what you want and don't want out of life.

The point is we are all here for a reason, to serve some purpose, and although you may not know what your purpose is at the moment, it still doesn't take away from the importance of your existence. Start asking yourself what do you love to do? Then simply start doing it. Guessing at what you are meant to become is no fun but when you know what you're bound to become life becomes even more awesome. So create the life you want, with the life you already have inside you.

FOCUS, & IT WILL COME INTO BEING

What you choose to focus on will determine how your life will form. So if you never focus on what you want in life prepare to tell your story of what you always wanted in life. Therefore, you must continually keep your goals in focus and move towards them.

The United States one hundred-dollar bill features Pennsylvania's 6th President Benjamin Franklin. A man who grew up poor with 16 siblings, with only two years of formal education. But somehow he still managed to be one of the primary founders of the University of Pennsylvania in 1740, and contributed to America gaining its independence on July 4, 1776, invented many inventions such as the lightening rod, bifocal glasses, and the glass armonica just to name a few. But how did he achieve such great things? Simple, he knew how to direct his focus.

See when we concentrate we are forced to observe and focus our mind on one object. But when our attention is scattered we are forced to re-group, re-adjust, and re-focus our un-concentrated attention. Truth is every act, skill or goal needs its own proper dose of attention in order for it to be carried out successfully. Think about it driving, writing, cooking and cleaning all require us to focus in order for us to perform them successfully.

So, in order for our ability to focus to be useful, it must be regulated by our will to pay attention. You have to be able to decide when and where to focus your mind, especially when it comes to the center of your interest. This is why we will always fail at big things if we're constantly getting distracted by small things, because it's so easy to lose focus in a world full of distractions.

Professional boxer Archie Moore would have never had 131 knockouts if he would have never focused. Moore's ability to accomplish this is a great example of how life is similar to a camera; because when we decide to focus on what we're trying to capture, we have an amazing ability to bring those images to life. So discontinue directing your mental energy towards things of little to no value that are non-beneficial to you and your purpose.

Instead, practice giving all of your goals, all of your undivided attention. Make it a habit to concentrate on the relationship between your heart and your mind in order to generate healthy levels of clarity, fulfillment and peace. Because when you have mental lucidity, any obstacle you face will not entangle your judgement because you are focused and able to think therefore the path before you is illuminated. However, when clarity is absent, so is ones focus, and the mind will have trouble remaining calm as it will be left scrambling trying to figure out what to do next.

So you will either be the boss of what you decide to focus on or what you decide to focus on will remain the boss of you. Which should give you even more of a reason to silence the noise around you and focus!

DON'T LIMIT YOUR DREAMS, DREAM WITHOUT LIMITS

During the time it was still illegal to teach slaves how to read and write. A young Booker T. Washington found himself growing up on a plantation in which he described as "The most miserable, desolate, and discouraging surroundings."[1] As him and three of his siblings were forced to sleep on filthy rags laid out on a dirt floor, Washington was determined to educate himself after he saw several dozen boys and girls sitting in a classroom one morning engaged in their studies.

This left such a lasting impression on him that in 1871 nine years after the Emancipation Proclamation was signed he saw "A young colored man among a large

---

[1] Washington, B. T. (1963). *Booker T. Washington up from slavery: An autobiography*. Garden City, NY: Doubleday

number of colored people, reading a newspaper" this fired up his ambition even more to learn how to read. So during his employment at the salt furnace with his stepfather he noticed how every barrel of salt that was packed in the mines was marked, and by watching the letters that were put on the salt barrels he eventually learned how to read.

As time went on Booker T. Washington was eventually able to put himself through school and became a teacher. He founded the Tuskegee Normal and Industrial Institute in Alabama in 1881, now known as Tuskegee University, and was awarded an honorary master's degree from Harvard University and an honorary doctorate from Dartmouth College in 1901 for his contributions to American society. That same year he also became the first African-American to be invited to the White House and became very close with President Theodore Roosevelt. Because Booker T. Washington didn't just dream he dreamed without limits.

Moreover, our dreams can't come into existence with our resistance. When we stand in the way of our aspirations it's a reflection of our intimidation to be successful. When we try to talk ourselves out of pursuing our dreams what we're really doing is talking ourselves into a nightmare of regret. The most disappointing conversation you could ever have with yourself is when you begin talking about all the things you could've been or could've done with your life.

In fact, the main two reasons why so many people hate their jobs is because they either had no idea what they wanted to do with their lives at the time so they settled for the routine 9-5. Or, they knew what they wanted to pursue in life but they never overcame their fear of taking a chance and reaching for their dreams so they simply put them on hold, placed them on the back burner and forgot about them. Instead, we should dream big, then begin dreaming even bigger. One of the key principles to dreaming without limits is remembering that you are where you are, because of how you think and the choices you've made thus far. So if you think negative, you'll behave negative, and speak negative, and will most likely react negative because that's what negative people do.

However, if you amend this way of thinking your thoughts will become more positive and so will your self-confidence. There's no better time to start doing what you love, so that you can begin loving what you do. So as seconds turn to minutes, and minutes turn to hours, and hours turn into days, you still have a chance to take advantage of new opportunities to make your dreams come true because each day is a new day to change your life, if you truly desire to.

If you want to succeed in life, you have to believe that you can or else you'll be really successful being unsuccessful. So no matter how big or small your dreams are, tell your brain to follow your feet and chase them. Identify the things you're great at, then use your gift to make an impact. Forget choosing a career based on what other people think, it's your life, walk in your purpose and follow your dreams and maybe those same people will begin to change how they think and start following theirs.

FIND A PROBLEM AND SOLVE IT

As long as people have problems they will always pay for solutions. In 2004, when Janet Jackson had a wardrobe malfunction at Super Bowl 38, who knew that it would inspire three friends to develop a video sharing website where anyone in the world could upload and watch videos around the clock 24 hours a day, 7 days a week, non-stop? After more than 100 million people saw Janet's unexpected "nip-slip" it not only became a topic of discussion on every news and radio broadcast but it also became a part of Jawed Karim's goal to find and view the footage online himself, since he had not seen it.

But he would soon discover that the footage was arduous to find. His friends Chad and Steve also found it frustrating that they could not share and view footage of a dinner party due to e-mail attachment limitations. So to solve this problem Jawed, Steve and Chad all began working on a website that would revolutionize how we broadcast ourselves. A year and half later they would sell it to Google for $1.65 billion and the rest is history.

Today, YouTube has more than 1 billion unique monthly visitors, over 300 hours of video is uploaded per minute, with more than 4 billion video views per day, and over 6 billion hours of video being watched per month. There is no denying that Youtube is a force to be reckoned with. The dynamic trio all found a problem and solved it, and someone obviously paid them for it. Now, YouTube is the hub of viral marketing, music, sports, entertainment, education and so much more. With this in view, we should never neglect our gifts but rather embrace them and use them to transform our world.

Your gift is your power, but most importantly it's the key that opens up the door to your destiny and entrepreneurs are aware of this. Think about it, Google which is almost everyone's favorite search engine, made search easy, even the phrase "Just Google it" has become the norm. Google now processes over 40,000 search queries each second on average, which equates to over

3.5 billion searches per day and more than 1.2 trillion searches per year according to Google search statistics.

We also can't forget ebay which simplified online buying and selling. Netflix introduced online entertainment on demand, including hundreds of movies, documentaries and dozens of popular TV shows. Uber made on-demand car service better while giving people an opportunity to make money being an independent contractor as an Uber driver. Today Uber is worth more than $60 billion dollars all because entrepreneur Travis Kalanick had an idea to create a mobile app that connects passengers with drivers for hire.

So ask yourself, what problems can you solve? What can you improve or make better? Entertainment executive Fred Freston once said "Innovation is taking two things that already exists, and putting them together in a whole new way." This alone should give us even more of a reason to tap into our ability to create wealth for ourselves utilizing the gifts we were born with. Because our gift is our key to our success.

Therefore, it must be understood by all that a key is used as an instrument to disengage a lock, so when you refuse to use your gift, you lock yourself out of fulfilling your purpose. The same way that a janitor has many keys, to open many doors to many rooms. Well, your gift has the same power, as it has the ability to help you unlock many doors of opportunity that can lead you down a very rewarding, fulfilling and meaningful path in life. So use your gift to find a problem and fix it or someone else will be getting paid for a problem you could have solved but didn't fix.

THE ENGINEERING OF GREATNESS

The engineering of greatness is the artful programming of one's ability to go above and beyond the norm. As inhabitants of the earth we're all designed to grow into our greatness considering the fact that we're all given free will to become the best version of ourselves. It's just that many of us haven't taken out the mandatory time to discover who we truly are. Once we do, only then will we realize what lies within. We would no longer remain confused about our lives nor the direction it's going in ultimately becoming aware that our passion is what drives us to our purpose. Once this is discovered our craving to be who we were born to be, will grow rapidly.

One of the most important rules to achieving personal happiness is to do what you love in life by turning your dreams into reality. But what I've discovered overtime is that all dreams require fuel to produce power, especially dreams that have the potential to transform lives.

The same way an internal combustion engine requires a proper ratio of air and gasoline to perform properly. Well the composition of our aspirations operate in a similar fashion because they require a constant supply of energy, and effort to gain momentum. In other words, our dreams need the proper dose of planning, preparing, and practice when in pursuit of them. Once we are cognizant of this we tap into our ability to unlock our greatness and can truly push the limits of our imagination. Therefore, a dream without ambition is like a car without fuel, you'll go nowhere fast!

So, right now, in this very moment, ask yourself— what kind of statement do you want to make with your life? In what ways will you leave your mark and be remembered? There are so many individuals on this planet who are real-life demonstrations that we can be anything we desire to be, within the parameters of our natural abilities.

But before we try to embrace our greatness, we must first release all negative energy from our way of thinking. Because everything that manifests itself into our lives is there because it matches the vibration of our thoughts. Everything that we can see, hear, taste, smell and touch is a result of energy. Therefore, when the brain translates what we see, hear, taste, smell and touch it perceives it as being our reality. So the minute you can change how you look at yourself and your circumstance, both you and your circumstance will begin to change.

In 1872, when Henry Royce's father passed away at the tender age of 9, Royce had to start working in order to contribute to his family's household income. He accomplished this by selling newspapers and delivering telegrams. By the time he turned 15, he had completed only one year of school and officially became an elementary school dropout.

But who knew that years later in 1901 after buying a used French built—10HP two-cylinder Decauville that Henry Royce would be inspired to improve upon its design and build his own line of cars by hand. It is said that he was determined to build the best motor car in the world regardless of what it would cost. So in 1906, Royce, along with co-founder and friend Charles Rolls, would both become two of the world's most creative pioneers of automotive engineering. Today, Rolls-Royce manufactures one of the most exquisite luxury brand automobiles that money can buy. In fact, a Rolls-Royce Phantom alone can easily cost upward of $500,000, with its iconic proportions and timeless elegance, followed by its twin-turbo 6.6-liter 563 horsepower V-12 engine, with rich leather seating and handsomely crafted wood veneers.

Royce was not only an engineering genius, he was ahead of his time. He knew how significant he was and therefore choose to walk in his purpose regardless of his formal education, situation or circumstance. He was known to be a very hard worker who never stopped working and not once did he allow his lack of education stand in his way. As a result he managed to embody the true meaning of greatness.

CREATE THE LIFE YOU WANT

The next time you find yourself complaining about how you're not where you want to be in life remember that the only sure way of living the kind of life you want is by simply using your mind to create it. In fact, your motivation will become stronger when you have a clear vision of what you want to achieve. You also begin to realize that you're in charge of your own future and that nothing will be handed to you.

Sadly, we've all seen the damaging effects of poverty and how it can weaken a nation, communities, families, and children. But what many people don't see, is how growing up in a low-income family that struggled to make ends meet can hinder the mind, and deter you from achieving your goals in life.

But just because you may have been a victim of economic hardship growing up doesn't mean you have remain stuck in a poverty-stricken mentality going forward, into your future. That's right, growing up underprivileged, doesn't mean you have to stay underprivileged, because staying poor is a choice. We often point fingers and blame others for where we are in life only to forget that there are three fingers pointing back at us whenever we point ours. Where we are in life is nobody's fault but our own. So if you don't like the direction your life is going in, keep making all the turns you can until it finally turns out the way that is pleasing to you.

What must be understood and kept at the forefront of our minds is that greatness lies within us all. But we must first take full responsibility for the decisions we've made in our lives and accept the consequences that have followed. This means taking full responsibility for every level of your life including your education level, achievement level, income level, health level, debt level, success level, and most importantly, your level of happiness.

When you take full responsibility for your life you eliminate all excuses, own up to all your actions, and admit to all of your mistakes. It means no more playing the victim, and no more using your "shoulda, coulda, woulda's" as a crutch. Creating the life that you want is also about moving beyond your pain and into your purpose in order to enjoy the things that make you happy.

As a former drug addict, ex-gang banger and convict, famous actor Danny Trejo is a real-life demonstration of what it means to create the kind of life you want. He was in and out of prison for 11 years of his life and even escaped the death penalty. Trejo was kept in solitary confinement for three months at Soledad correctional facility and was facing the gas-chamber for allegedly throwing a rock at a lieutenant during a prison riot. But due to a technicality in his case the charges were later dropped. It was at that moment that Trejo decided to change his life forever. He says, "I knew my life would be over if I didn't make changes to it. So I prayed, and vowed to change, and to get sober." But before the change, and before the fame, Trejo lived a life of armed robberies, shootouts, selling and using drugs, and even stashed $7,000 in his mother's backyard after selling seven ounces of sugar to a federal agent—talk about a real life movie! But Trejo did his time in prison and is now doing time in Hollywood on the red carpet. He currently has over 270 movies under his belt including films such as Desperado, Spy Kids, and his most infamous film yet, Machete, which grossed over $44 million at the box office.

Trejo never gave up on creating the life he wanted for himself—and now he has it. He didn't make excuses, he just started making wiser choices. He didn't use his past to beat himself down; instead he embraced opportunity whenever it came around. He even became a drug counselor after his last stint in 1969 and he often meets with various groups in various prisons to share his story of triumph to **demonstrate that there's still hope to** turn your life around. He is definitive proof that we all have the ability to create the life we desire. We just need to learn how to use constructive energy, followed by constructive action, to form a more constructive life.

TURNING YOUR IDEAS INTO A BUSINESS

Coming up with great ideas may be easy for some. But putting those ideas into action can be challenging for many. However, for Gary Dahl this wasn't the case. Because he was the creator of a very silly, yet very successful idea in the 70's that made him a fortune. His idea was a Pet Rock. Yes, an ordinary rock that you can dig up in almost anyone's backyard.

The Pet Rock was to serve as your new pet that you'd never need to feed, walk, bathe, groom or neuter. It would also come in a cardboard box stuffed with bedding material to keep your new Pet Rock cozy and warm, and although some came with a leash you'd never have to worry about your new pet rock running away—

ever! But what Dahl originally meant as a joke while talking with his friends at a bar one night turned out to be a very lucrative idea, an idea that made him $15 million richer in just six short months. So this should give you even more of a reason to turn your ideas into a business.

The founder of Virgin Mobile, Richard Branson once explained that, "Any idea can be a great idea, if you dream big, think differently, and commit to seeing it be released." So regardless of how good or bad you think your ideas may sound, write them down. Next, take out the time to do some market research on them. This will ultimately help you to decide whether it's appealing or not, learn who your target audience is, who your competition is and how well they're performing.

You may also want to look into setting aside a very small budget to test your ideas. But that's only if you feel that there's a need for your product or service in the market. This can be done by simply buying a domain name, or creating a Facebook fan page to help grow your idea, or you can do both by setting up a website where people can buy your products or services online. Finally, don't be afraid to dip your new idea into the pool of marketing, by testing it with Google Adwords, Bing, or Yahoo advertising. The goal is to see how many people are curious enough to at least click on your link and go to your website, and at what conversion rate.

You should also make it a habit to study your competition's products or services and the overall quality of their products or services. Then see if you can sell yours at a cheaper price without compromising on the elements of its quality. Moreover, continue to learn as much as you possibly can about your competition including all of their up and coming projects, changes and releases.

Although this takes time, energy, and effort, this is how you win in business. Sadly enough, most ideas remain dormant because most people don't make time to manifest them, or they may not have the money or contacts to start them. But this is why you must apply your mind and grind. Bringing your ideas to life is very similar to giving birth to a child. You have to push for it, attend to it, care for it, cater to it, mold it, but most importantly, you have to nurture it.

Furthermore, the art of believing and achieving in business is understanding that business is a matter of skill, knowledge and application. But skill, knowledge and application can only be mastered by training, experience and practice. So turning your ideas into a business can turn your fears into courage when you apply these proficiencies. By dominating your fears, you allow fearlessness to dominate you.

You should also outline your business goals by writing a formal business plan. This will help you steer your business in the right direction, and will help lenders and investors see your vision for your organization if your business idea grows to that point. It's almost like a blueprint of how you will achieve your company's goals. You should also look into signing up for business workshops, seminars and classes that are offered at your local Small Business Development Center, also known as SCORE; you can do this by logging onto www.score.org.

You will then need to decide if you want to operate out of a physical location, or if you want to be based online, or both. You should also look into consulting with a business lawyer who can help educate you on the myriad of legal issues that can confront any organization. He or she can help assist you to review any and all legal contracts, help create employment policies, and aid with any legal questions or concerns that you may have. They will also help you to decide which legal entity would fit you and your company best, such as a sole proprietorship, S-Corp, C-Corp, partnership, corporation, or a limited liability company (LLC), because they're all different in structure in the eyes of the law.

Next, decide what you would like your business name to be, and register your trade name, also known as a "Doing Business As" (DBA) by going to www.sba.gov. You'll then need to apply for a business Tax ID number, also known as an EIN number, from the IRS website. This helps the IRS identify business taxpayers. Lastly, apply for any and all applicable permits and licenses that are required in your state to ensure that you are in compliance with the law before you operate your business to avoid any fines and penalties.

THE TRUTH ABOUT BUSINESS

If starting a business was easy there's a high possibility that everyone would be trying to start one. However, it's not, and in fact it can be quite challenging. What most people fail to tell you is that if you're expecting to make boatloads of cash in the beginning stages of running a start-up, sorry but you're in for a rude awakening. Because the ugly truth of start-up growth is that it can take years before a new business becomes profitable. In fact, most start-ups are not profitable for the first three to five years of being in business, and about 50% of them fail within that time frame.

Square, Inc. for example, the secure credit card mobile processing app, started in 2009, with $300 million in venture capital. However, it's been burning through a great deal of cash ever since. Its founder, Jack

Dorsey, who is also the co-founder of Twitter, is one of the biggest and most ambitious innovators of our time. Yet, his latest venture has been having some trouble staying afloat with its long history of losses. After borrowing more than $100 million from Goldman Sachs, Morgan Stanley, J.P. Morgan and Barclays in 2013, they managed to persuade investors to pour another $340 million into the startup in 2014; and in 2015 they were able to raise another $150 million in investor funding with a $6 billion valuation. But despite all their efforts the company has still not managed to yield a profit, despite their current rate of growth.

Perhaps this is why business experts highly suggest that you're better off buying an existing business that's already profitable with a proven track record of sales. The reason being is that these types of businesses have already established themselves in the marketplace, have learned from their mistakes, and built a strong clientele base. In addition, customers who are already familiar with an existing company's product or service proves that there is an existing market ready, willing and able to pay for them. However, this doesn't mean that a start-up will not be successful, because many have been; it just means that an existing business with a proven sales record has a higher chance of continuing to be lucrative.

Truth is, starting a new business is like jumping out of an airplane with the materials to make a parachute. And on the way down you're in a race against time to stitch it together to release it before you land and hit the ground. Yes, it can be fun, exciting, and very rewarding, but at the same time being an entrepreneur can be very demanding, stressful, and exhausting, because you're in a never-ending battle with uncertainty. When starting a business, you have to make money, because money is what's required in order to keep your business moving forward. So here are a few tips you may want to consider before embarking on the path of entrepreneurship.

1. Document

Write down all of your operating costs before you get started, such as your overhead, equipment, inventory, and marketing materials, as well as any fixtures and licenses that may be required of you.

2. Staff

Will you have employees? If so, how many? How much are you willing to pay them hourly? Add these numbers up; this will be your labor costs.

3. Insurance
All states require that you purchase workers compensation insurance once you have an employee on payroll. So you must factor in the cost of this as well. Rates vary by state.

4. Experiment
Prepare to test different marketing strategies. But also prepare to fail, because not all of them will work. However, don't be discouraged because this only prepares you for what eventually will work.

5. Funding
Are you taking out a business loan? If so, what will your monthly payments be? This is important, because you must add this into your monthly operating costs as well.

The Art of Believing & Achieving

6. Living Expenses

Add up all of your personal bills. This includes your rent/mortgage, car note, auto insurance, credit cards, phone bill, cable bill, student loans, gym membership, food and entertainment, and any other bill you can think of. This is will play an intricate role in helping you to decide if you can currently afford to put the time, hustle and effort into your business idea.

7. Your Grand Total

Now, add up the total cost of all of your operating expenses and your living expenses. This will be the grand total of what you will need to generate each month in order to stay in business and maintain your current standard of living.

So let's say that your business and living expenses come out to be a grand total of $3,500 a month. You will need to divide $3,500 by the cost of your product or service, then divide that number by 30, because there's normally 30 days in a month. For example, let's say you plan to sell cups of coffee at $5 a cup. This means you'll need to divide $3,500 by $5 which gives you a total of 700. So you will need to sell at least 700 cups of coffee a month, which equates to about 23-24 cups of coffee a day that you will need to sell just to cover both your business and living expenses. Keep in mind that this does not include any profit after all expenses have been paid.

However, every cup of coffee you'd sell thereafter would essentially be your net income, or better known as your "take home pay." This is one of the primary reasons why it takes businesses years before they become profitable; they have to consistently build up their clientele so that their products or services can continue to sell, which helps their business not fail.

Moreover, going into business for yourself requires an enormous investment of your time, energy, and effort. So when an entrepreneur doesn't have a clear vision then he or she will move in different directions wasting a lot of time, effort, energy & money. The end result is total frustration and possibly financial ruin. And it's also common to actually lose a lot of money before you actually start earning it, and sometimes you won't earn anything at all.

Regardless, you have to be determined to do whatever it takes to build and establish your company's vision and mission. But most importantly, you want to create a system that will turn your business into something bigger, a system that can be repeated by trained workers until it eventually grows and runs independent of you. This is how true entrepreneurs think and work.

VALUE IS IN THE EYE OF THE BEHOLDER

When celebrity photographer Kevin Abosch sold a simple portrait of an organic Irish potato to a European business man, he reportedly sold it to him for $1.08 million. Abosch says that after having two glasses of wine the wealthy man said, "I really like that picture." After two more glasses, Abosch told the BBC that the business man began to express his strong interest in the picture even more. Two weeks later, they agreed on a price, and the portrait of an Irish potato was sold for seven figures. Abosch said it was the most he's been paid for a piece of work that wasn't commissioned.

Like beauty, value is in the eye of the beholder. So what you cherish and believe is valuable may not be cherishable or valuable to someone else. The truth is, a consumer's "perceived value" of a good or service determines the price that he or she is willing to pay for it. Just the other day I read an article that reported how Babe Ruth's New York Yankees jersey sold for $4.4 million at a sports auction, setting a new world record for the highest sale price for a piece of sports memorabilia.

The world is full of things that attract our attention, and stimulate our senses. How attractive the item is to the eye, and how it feels to us on the inside, helps us to decide what we feel something is worth. For instance, we've been conditioned to believe that gold is steadier in value than any other metal and that it supposedly supports our world currency. Although it's been proven that there isn't enough gold in the earth to back our monetary system, we still choose to be convinced that gold symbolizes wealth.

When in reality gold doesn't produce earnings or dividends, and although many banks and investors own gold bars and coins, you can't eat or drink gold bars and coins in a famine. If the world suddenly had a shortage of food, and you didn't have anymore, but you had all the gold in the world in your treasure chest, would you trade all your gold for a hot plate of food? Or better yet, do you think someone would be willing to trade a portion of their food for your gold? Something that would not keep them alive and provide them with nourishment? So at that point how valuable is your gold?

As a society, we put a value on almost everything. We value food because we want to live. We value shelter because we don't want to be exposed to the harsh elements of nature. We value water because our body needs it to survive; we put a value on education because we believe that getting a diploma or a degree will take us further in life; we put a value on our relationships, cars, homes, and money, because the idea of value has always been created by nothing more than our own human imaginations.

INVENT THE FUTURE

Computer scientist Alan Curtis Kay once said, "The best way to predict the future is to invent it." On November 12, 1990 that's what British engineer and computer scientist Tim Berners-Lee set his mind to do when he wrote a two-phase proposal to invent what is now known as the World Wide Web. This interconnected system of information would allow people from across the globe to communicate with anyone, from anywhere, at any time, as long as they had a computer and an internet connection.

This system would also enable people to share documents, graphics, video and audio files without restrictions via email or live chat. Berners-Lee designed this global network so that we could have access to unlimited amounts of information at our disposal, at all times. Today, over 7 billion people access the internet worldwide, with more than 1 billion registered websites, and more than 100 billion emails being sent out each day. Now it is officially the world's fastest growing communication system, considering that it took only five years for the internet to achieve its first 50 million users, whereas television took 13 years and radio took 38.

As the power of the internet continues to grow at a rapid pace, no one can deny how it has changed our society, our education system, our lives, and more importantly the world at large. It revolutionized how we communicate, date, shop, travel, bank, promote, and perform research. We can even enroll in online college courses.

In fact, many people have even gone so far as quitting their jobs to become their own boss from the comfort of their own home. The Web has also allowed us to trade stocks for a living or during our leisure from our mobile devices, without us ever having to be on the trading floor on Wall Street. We can search and apply for jobs, read news, find entertainment, download music, and best of all we can keep in touch with our friends and family by simply logging onto our Facebook, Twitter, Instagram, Vine, Snapchat, Pinterest, and Periscope accounts—daily.

The Internet has made a huge impact on society, and if it weren't for Berners-Lee, the World Wide Web might not exist in the form we have come to know it in. This means that company sites like Google, Yahoo, eBay, Tumblr, Amazon, Facebook, Twitter, YouTube, iTunes, Expedia, Netflix, and every other dot com registry may not exist in the form we have come to know them in as well. Berners-Lee created something we have grown to depend on, as the Internet has given these companies, and others like them, a platform to blossom into multi-billion dollar businesses.

I mean, where else can you make $1.6 billion in a single day? Founder and creator of Facebook Mark Zuckerberg did, all due to the power of the Web. Thanks to Tim Berners-Lee and his innovation, we can search for new and used vehicles on sites like Autotrader and Cars.com. We also have the luxury of searching for hotels, houses and apartments anywhere in the world on sites like Hotels.com, Realtor.com and Apartments.com.

And let's not forget our magical search engines that give us the answers to practically any question we ask.

It also wouldn't be as easy to sell things if it weren't for the Web. Sites like eBay, Amazon, and Craigslist allow us to create and post ads, and help us sell some of our most prized possessions for a little extra cash. Where else can you sell a 1978 Cessna airplane to a pair of $5 sandals? All on one site, with just a click of a button?

So let us not take for granted the impact we can make with our lives if we simply choose to be impactful because we all have the ability to shape the world around us, just like Berners-Lee did and many others before and after him. We are all capable of sculpting our corner of the world in either constructive or destructive ways, giving us a copious amount of power to consciously make our future brighter or dimmer. So I encourage you to go out into the world and use your power to help others recognize theirs.

You see, the whole purpose of human creation is manifestation. Our lives are just a duration of time that has been given to us to make a difference in the world. But the only way to make this difference is by exerting new ideas, concepts, and solutions. So dedicate your time to what gives your life meaning, because in the end, we all have the ability to dream up what has yet to come.

BE CREATIVE

Creativity is the utilization of our imagination to materialize our ideas to make our own reality. Just like any other skill, creativity can be learned, practiced, and developed. Photography takes practice, so does singing, coding, graphic design and drawing. Learning to be more creative is no different. In fact, your creativity will begin to blossom when you push yourself outside of your comfort zone and begin learning something new. For instance, try signing up for salsa lessons, or a culinary class, or perhaps consider learning a new instrument, and watch your creative energy begin to swell.

Learning new skills also helps with keeping your mind sharp, improves memory and can help fight off dementia. Psychologist Scott Barry Kaufman says, "Challenging activities help strengthen interacting brain regions within the brain." Being creative also means giving yourself the freedom to make mistakes, without being hard on yourself. This means giving yourself the privilege to be open, playful, and risky, with certain ideas and concepts.

For example, since 2013, China has been in the process of building artificial islands and military bases in the South China Sea, at a fast pace. They're doing this by dumping sand on coral reefs. So far they've managed to construct about 2,900 acres of land, with the help of dredgers to finish the project. Today, ships and planes can actually dock there and land. Although the project is currently undergoing a lot of scrutiny there's no denying that from a creative standpoint it's a true work of art—especially once you Google the images.

Lastly, psychologist and author Edward de Bono says that, "Creativity involves breaking out of established patterns in order to look at things in a different way." So remember without creativity we wouldn't have computers, television, cell phones, automobiles and so on, because that's what's needed in life if we want to see our ideas come to life.

EXPECT PROBLEMS

According to Murphy's Law, if anything can go wrong, then it most likely will at the worst possible time, all the time, all at once. But then Charles Swindoll reminds us that "Life is 10% of what happens to us, and 90% is how we respond to it." Therefore, the only thing that we can control is how we react to a dilemma requiring a fundamental solution. In business especially, problems are just inescapable, because businesses are always changing, growing and evolving. Customers make demands, and companies try to meet those demands; customers make complaints, and businesses look for ways to resolve those complaints.

Sometimes your workers may not perform their hired task and duties, so a supervisor or a manager may have to go behind them and do it themselves; or sometimes your top performer quits on you, and you're left scrambling to replace them with someone who's just as good. Even worse sometimes a new shipment may not get delivered on time and you're left stuck for a few days trying to think of ways that will help keep the traffic flowing in and out of your business until it finally arrives.

Award-winning business journalist Jonathan Berr knows about businesses and some the problems they face. He once reported in the Fiscal Times that the CEO of Radio Shack, Joe Magnacca, had vowed to transform the entire business due to the depletion of sales. He wrote, "Radio Shack has been struggling to keep pace with technology and stave off fiscal oblivion for years. In 1999, the shares sold for $78.50. Now, they sell for $2.66. The company has seen its market capitalization shrink by 98 percent. It now has a value of $270.4 million, which is tiny for a national retail chain."

Although problems can sometimes bring about meaningful changes, it's certainly unrealistic to expect to live without them—especially in business. Many people think that once you make it to the top, or once their business is successful, they can relax. But it's actually the exact opposite. Once you begin to succeed, the entrepreneurial path only becomes more challenging. Sure, certain aspects like making more money gets easier. You dress better, look better, and eat at better restaurants. But like many millionaires and billionaires have discovered it's easy to run into problems because you'll never run out of them. Therefore, the key is to navigate your way out of them and not let your problems keep you down. Instead, use them to help you get going and apply creative solutions to keep you going.

LEARN

Learn from your mistakes, your failures, and from the people around you. Learn as much as you can about yourself, about wealth, and about foods that can help you stay in good health. Feed on knowledge, feast on wisdom, and digest understanding. Learn to believe, and you'll constantly achieve. Learn your purpose so that you can master your craft; and after you master your craft, take the first step on your assigned path. Learn to be patient, and understand the power of waiting because timing is everything when you're waiting to be in power. But you'll learn over time that great things happen when you least expect them.

Learn how to keep pushing when you feel you can't push anymore. Learn your strengths as well as your weaknesses; then learn how you can make each of them stronger and use them to your advantage. Learn how to maintain your focus, and you'll stay focused. Learn how to use the power of positivity and use it to conquer negativity.

Learn to meditate, and cleanse your mind from anything impure. Learn how to silence your thoughts in order to hear the sound of your soul. What is it telling you? And what is it trying to show you? Learn to be obedient to your purpose, and you'll learn how to purposely be obedient. Learn as much as you can about whatever it is you desire to learn, and most importantly, learn to apply it. Learn to accept your wrongs, because you won't always be right, and learn to appreciate the sun after persevering through your darkest nights. Learn!

COMMIT TO YOUR PURPOSE

When your purpose becomes the center of your attraction, that attraction becomes the center of your life. However, when you refuse to walk in it on purpose, you'll step right into someone else's. Expect to conform to their agenda, playing the part they want you to play, acting how they want you to act, and being how they want you to be. In fact, when you step into someone else's purpose, they will give you a set of instructions that will instruct you on how to fulfill their vision, mission, while paying you to forget yours. Sadly, this ultimately pushes you down the path of conformity and forces you to depart from your true goals and aspirations.

For some reason our society has always narrowed down success to a checklist. We are told to go to school and to get an education, go to college and get a degree, find a job, and then work on finding ways to climb the corporate ladder. We are then encouraged to put money into a 401K and hang on for the next 20 years until we are able to retire at age 62—what an amazing life!

Now, by all means, if these are your goals and aspirations in life, then I'm not talking to you. But if you're anything like me and believe that you've been placed on this earth to live out your true purpose and your true area of excellence, then continue to strive, and do whatever it takes morally and ethically to make your dreams come alive.

Know that your life is infused with meaning and it is intended to impart a message that will encourage others to find the meaning of their lives. If you can remember this it will ultimately help your life become more fulfilling, and certainly more rewarding. Can't you see that walking in your purpose is the whole purpose of living? But if you don't commit to it you become unfaithful to your intended mission, and begin having an affair with someone else's vision. This is why staying committed to your dreams is so important; because when you fail to commit to your dreams, your dreams will most certainly fail to come true. So no matter what circumstance you find yourself in, always believe in yourself and commit to what you want to do in life. Concentrate, and put your heart into it, because the world depends on you; and as a whole, we depend on each other.

Singers and songwriters all know that music is medicine for the soul, and can serve as many things such as motivation, inspiration, and meditation. Because music is therapeutic it heals the heart, and has the ability to relax the mind. Think of all the Beyoncé, Taylor Swift and Adele fans who constantly wait for them to release new music. This is because all of their fans depend on the singers' purpose, which is to make good music.

So whatever your purpose is, devote yourself to it and concentrate on the fact that it's a constant thing that you've been put here to do permanently. Your purpose is designed to affect the people around you, and the people around them, and is intended to make history within and beyond your generation.

French virologist Françoise Barré-Sinoussi was the first scientist to discover the HIV virus, which has now infected more than 1.2 million people in the United States alone. Barré-Sinoussi stated that she is now making it her duty to get other researchers, worldwide, to work together to treat and prevent this infectious disease from spreading further. Hopeful, confident, and sanguine about the future; so many people infected with this virus are relying on Barré-Sinoussis' and her colleagues research because of the impact their purpose can make in this world.

See, the truth is each day we depend on what each of us are naturally gifted at. Think about it, When we show signs and symptoms of an illness we rely on the purpose of our doctors; when we need work done on our teeth we rely on the purpose of our dentist; if there's a fire we depend on the purpose of our firefighters; if we're in trouble with the law we depend on the purpose of a lawyer; and when we're in need of emergency assistance we rely on the purpose of 9-1-1. Why? Because all things begin and end with purpose.

DO WHAT YOU LOVE

Do what you love and you'll never have to worry about leaving for work in the morning at eight, to spend the next eight hours doing what you hate. If there's one thing that makes us avoid pursuing our dreams, it's the fear of not being able to take care of our families, and most importantly ourselves. This fear is what keeps us working in unfulfilling jobs—because we enjoy the security of a paycheck. But the truth is, no job is secure. From a business perspective, if a company is failing to make money and sales are continuing to decline it's more than likely they're going to look for ways to cut costs and will eventually begin making cuts by letting people go.

This is why I prefer to travel the road less traveled, which is the road of entrepreneurship. Despite there being so much to learn, I love being in charge of my own destiny. But this road is not an easy one to travel, especially with fear, risk, and uncertainty constantly lurking in the corners of your mind. It can be extremely rewarding on one hand, and extremely overwhelming on the other. And if you can't handle pressure you'll fold. I've also learned very quickly along the way that making one bad business decision can lead to a total loss of invested capital, either in whole or in part, which can ultimately cause a huge financial set-back and lead to the total demise of your company. And in some cases, the complete loss of your own personal savings.

This is another reason why so many people never start a business and opt out of doing what they're passionate about—because it's just too risky. Entrepreneurship is a day-to-day grind, and in the beginning stages you may not make a dime. But as they say, if you wouldn't do it for free, then you shouldn't do it at all, and you certainly shouldn't do it just for the money. Instead, focus on doing what you love and you'll never have to work a day in your life doing what you hate. Influential painter Vincent Van Gogh is a real-life demonstration of what it means to love what you do, and do what you love. During his lifetime, he managed to draw approximately 900 paintings, and 1,100 total drawings and sketches combined.

However, he only sold one painting during his entire existence, and he only became famous after his death. Sadly, Van Gogh will never experience the joy of knowing that the painting he once painted in June 1890 of a peasant woman against a background of wheat was sold for $47.5 million to billionaire Steve Wynn, CEO of Wynn Resorts.

Van Gogh is considered to be one of the greatest painters to have ever lived, and has had an immeasurable amount of influence on art culture, but the truth is he died with not a penny to his name. However, he was still determined to do what he enjoyed doing best—paint. Many people are unaware of the fact that he often went without food and lived in poverty. But he never allowed a lack of money or food to stand in the way of doing what her loved and what he felt gave him personal fulfillment.

His story also teaches us that doing what you love awakens you from within. It is a burning desire that intensifies the more it is utilized. All too often, we trick ourselves into believing that success is contingent on the amount of money we make; but this is far from the truth, because success is nothing more than a state of mind that helps build the foundation of our future.

So try spending some time in solitude identifying what you really want to do in life. This sense of personal fulfillment is priceless regardless of whether you make money from it or not, although that's the goal. Because like Steve Jobs once said "The only way to do great work is to love what you do. If you haven't found it yet, keep looking. Don't settle."

IS COLLEGE FOR YOU?

There comes a time in our lives when we must ask ourselves if pursuing a college degree is right for us. On one hand, studies show that a college degree leads to higher earnings; but on the other, over 260,000 graduates made above or below the federal minimum wage level of $7.25 per hour in 2013, according to the Bureau of Labor Statistics. In addition, the average 2016 college graduate holds $37,172 in student loan debt, according to student loan expert Mark Kantrowitz.

Normally, the average graduate would have to work anywhere between 8-10 years before their student loans are paid in full. However, new research shows that the average bachelor's degree holder now takes almost 21 years to pay back their student loans.

Moreover, a number of studies carried out over the years have shown that individuals with college degrees earn significantly more annually, compared to those with just a high school diploma or a GED. But with the cost of college tuition skyrocketing, a degree no longer ensures an increase in one's earning power nor does it guarantee employment. In fact, the U.S. labor market still has a deficit of more than 7 million jobs, and the unemployment rate has been at 6.6 percent or higher for the last five-and-a-half years.

But it's still good to know that people with college degrees have a far easier time finding a job than those without. A person holding a Ph.D. for example can make anywhere from $37,286-202,281 a year depending on one's occupation. It's the highest degree you can earn, and they certainly don't come easy, nor are they cheap. Not only do you have to dedicate years of your life to earn it, you have to figure out a way to pay for it as well.

This means that you will need to find a job afterwards that pays you enough to make you feel that it was all worth it. The average student who graduates from medical school will acquire $166,750 of student loan debt. So let's say that it takes the student about 30 years to pay their loans back, with a 7.5% interest rate. Overtime, they will eventually end up paying a total cost of $419,738 after 30 years of accrued interest. So when we compare doctors to the average college graduate, doctors are almost half a million dollars in the hole by their early thirties.

But then, you have some of the richest people in the world who dropped out of college or skipped it all together and became extremely wealthy. Entrepreneur, and author Jim Rohn said it best "Formal education will make you a living, but self-education will make you a fortune." Just take the Swedish business magnate and founder of IKEA Ingvar Kampard, who is currently worth $3.4 billion, with no formal college education; the same can be said about Russell Simmons who is the co-founder of Def Jam records and Russell Simmons Music Group. He has managed to create massive wealth for himself without finishing college, and has an estimated net worth of $325 million.

The same can be said about Bill Gates co-founder of Microsoft, the world's largest software company, who is currently worth $79.4 billion. He dropped out of Harvard University just so he could focus on building Microsoft. So the decision to go to college is something only you can decide. It's a big commitment, comes with an expensive price tag and can leave you in a sea of debt. However, it looks good on your resume, has the potential to increase your earning potential, can provide job stability, and helps you be more marketable in the job market. So choose wisely.

THE ENTREPRENEURIAL MIND

Once an entrepreneur believes in their vision, they create a plan and make it their mission to push out that vision. One thing all successful entrepreneurs have in common is their keen eye for opportunity. Because when an entrepreneur looks at the world, their community, and their environment they view it differently than others because what he or she is constantly looking out for are business opportunities. For example, if a subdivision has no nearby supermarkets, a normal person would most likely complain about it not being any nearby supermarkets. However, an entrepreneur sees dollar signs, and an opportunity to open-up a profitable grocery store.

In the process, entrepreneurs have to take calculated risks while carefully managing themselves and others. The entrepreneur mind is a mind that formulates a winning strategy, which ultimately gives them a competitive advantage. In most cases, the entrepreneur mind finds something that's already working but they figure out a way to make it work better.

Since entrepreneurs are a unique breed of people, the entrepreneur mind sees challenges as opportunities. Where most people would begin to panic, an entrepreneur will most likely remain calm because their minds are trained to think reasonably under pressure. The entrepreneur mind also knows not to recklessly jump into a business venture. It does not make business decisions on a whim. The entrepreneur mind does its research first, conducts a study, and thinks things through before taking action. He or she also looks for smarter, and more efficient ways to accomplish everyday tasks.

The entrepreneur mind knows that without sales, business fails. So they make it habit to study marketing and try to think of clever ways to capture the consumer's attention by infusing humor into their content—creatively.

Moreover, as innovators and risk takers, entrepreneurs spark new industries, they discover new ways to enhance products and services, and they are the backbone of our nation's economy. In the book *Entrepreneur Mind: 100 Essential Beliefs, Characteristics, and Habits of Elite Entrepreneurs*, author Kevin D. Johnson does an outstanding job detailing the traits and thought patterns of an entrepreneur. He wrote:

"To be an entrepreneur is to think differently. While most people seek refuge, entrepreneurs take risks. They don't want a job; they want to create jobs. Their goal isn't to think outside the box as much as it is to own the box. Entrepreneurs don't follow the market; they define the market. This bold and seemingly backward way of thinking I refer to as the Entrepreneur Mind."

Furthermore, being an entrepreneur comes with a lot of responsibility because our families and the families of the people we employ are all depending on us to constantly generate income. Because the job of feeding our families is not getting any easier. Therefore, as an entrepreneur you must keep in mind that the people you hire are depending on you to make effective business decisions, they're depending on you to increase sales, to manage your companies spending, and most importantly the government depends on entrepreneurs to create jobs for the sake of economic development.

But in order to achieve these things and more, entrepreneurs have to stay ahead of the curve by learning as much as they can about their competitors, marketing, and how to convert leads. This way of thinking in the world of entrepreneurship are small fights that lead to big wins.

No one said entrepreneurship would be easy. I myself have had my share of struggles, financial losses and setbacks. But none of these hindrances stopped me from getting back up, because in my mind, I am the only one who can keep me down. In my mind, I am still undefeated and have no shame admitting that I failed my way to success, because I chose to focus on results and the income from outcome.

Lastly, the entrepreneur mind is an optimistic one, because positive thoughts can transform your world. The entrepreneur mind knows that each day it determines the direction it want's its company to go in. As a result you're responsible for achieving its short and long-term goals. As well as your company's financial statements, taxes, failures, and future successes. The truth is, anyone can start a business, but not everyone can start a business and be successful. Therefore, the entrepreneur mind understands the power of patience, perseverance and passion. Mastering these qualities not only give the entrepreneur an advantage but make it twice as hard for them to fail.

FIND A NEED

Wherever there's a need, there will always be a demand. So for those of you who want to start a profitable business, find a need and fill it. With an accretion of entrepreneurs, it's very important to devise a creative yet concise marketing plan that will yield you the highest return on your investment and help you to become the leading global provider in your industry. So think big! Your goal should be to become recognized as the top supplier in your trade, until you and your company become a household name. If you can achieve this, it's almost 99.9% guaranteed that you'll become an embodiment of success.

Consider high school dropout Amadeo Peter Giannini for example, the founder of what is now known as Bank of America. In the late 1800's Giannini saw a need that had to be met while he was working for a small bank in North Beach, California. He realized that they, and almost every other bank, were unwilling to lend out loans to hard working class citizens; only the rich, or those who owned businesses were qualified to borrow money.

Giannini also saw that loaning money to hard working class citizens would allow them to better themselves in ways they wouldn't have been able to if it weren't for the bank giving them the financial means to do so. Qualifying people for loans would ultimately allow them to buy new homes or they could start new businesses. So Giannini didn't waste any time. In October 1904 he started his own bank, called the Bank of Italy, by raising $150,000 from various sources. Within a year, the Bank of Italy had managed to generate over $600,000 in deposits from the working class, which is over $3.5 million in today's value of the American dollar.

But it wasn't until 1906 when a massive 7.9 earthquake shook San Francisco, California that Giannini would really make his mark. He saw an opportunity in the marketplace, a job that needed to be filled, and a city that was destroyed and needed to be rebuilt. After the earthquake, devastating fires followed that spread throughout the city for several days, leaving over 200,000 people homeless and the city in ruins.

However, Giannini was solicitous about the future condition of his city and he felt if he did not act in time the economic recovery of San Francisco would be fatal. So the very next day on April 19, 1906—despite his bank's building being destroyed—Giannini headed out to the docks to set up a temporary bank. He knew that people needed help right then and there, so he immediately began taking deposits and giving out loans to those in need, and to those who could rebuild the city. This included businesses and the working class. In fact, the Bank of Italy was the only bank at that time willing to lend its services to the public. Other banks wanted to stay closed for up to six months, fearing that their institutions wouldn't survive.

As word quickly spread about Giannini's bank offering assistance, so did the number of his bank locations. By 1917 he had already managed to open 292 more bank branches. In 1928 he finally changed the Bank of Italy's name to what we have all come to know today as Bank of America. He also became known for instituting a variety of practices that are still standard procedure in nearly all banks to this day. In fact, if it weren't for Giannini's practices, the gates of Disneyland would have never opened on July 17, 1955. Bank of America believed in Walt Disney and his vision to bring the magic and imagination of his cartoons to life. So they showed their support by investing $17 million to construct Disneyland under the direct supervision of Walt Disney himself. Bank of America also showed their support by sponsoring Disney's first animated movie, Snow White and the Seven Dwarfs, for $1.4 million.

Furthermore, when people struggle to get things done, this ultimately becomes a need that must be met, and as a result it becomes an opportunity for you to fill the need and create wealth for yourself. Today, Bank of America is worth more than $160 billion with over 5,000 branches across the U.S. Profiting from the 2006 financial crisis, they became one of the nation's largest financial institutions—all because one man saw a need that needed to be met, so he met it with a solution. As a result, Bank of Americas growth has accelerated rapidly as they continue to strengthen communities through lending, investing and charitable acts of contributions.

WHAT CAN YOU IMPROVE?

Today, I encourage you to write out a list of at least 10 things that you can do to help improve your overall quality of life. Maybe it's your health, attitude, communication skills, business, marriage, personal happiness, relationship or perhaps you just want to learn how to develop a more positive mindset. Whatever it is always remember that progress cannot be attained without change. So in order to live better, you have to think better to do better, or else you'll begin to believe that your life doesn't qualify to get better.

As an entrepreneur, speaking from the pulpit of my own experiences, I've always looked for ways to improve my business, and my customers' overall shopping experience when I had my clothing store, convenience store and beauty salon. I also made it my duty to respond to any and all issues or concerns that my customers may have had. When I had my clothing store in particular I remember always studying the type of clothing my customers would gravitate towards the most. I'd observe what caught their eye and what didn't, I'd analyze which items sold the most, and which items sold the least, compared to what didn't sell at all.

I would also take my customer's feedback into consideration and be open to any suggestions or recommendations that they may have had. Practicing this helped me to improve my business in so many ways.

So, in order to enhance any particular area of your life, identify all the things that you feel need to be improved upon and begin to work on them one-by-one. Also, learn to listen to what your heart and mind are telling you to do. Become better at mastering your energy. Reduce stress by organizing your priorities, and always take out the necessary time to reflect on your innermost personal thoughts and feelings, and any goals that you may have. Because this will help you spring those thoughts, feelings and goals into action. Practicing these basic techniques alone can help boost your confidence and make you more productive and awesome.

WHO WANTS TO BE A MILLIONAIRE?

Almost everyone has the potential to be a millionaire—even a six year old. Don't believe me? Just ask millionaire and former beauty pageant contestant Isabella Barrett, who runs her own business, Glitzy Girl, selling everything from silver diamond crown necklaces to glitzy $4 charms. She once told Mirror.co.uk, "What's not to like about being a millionaire?" She says, "I'm a superstar, I have my own jewelry line and I just love being the boss."

Furthermore, with so many different ways to become a millionaire nowadays, brilliant entrepreneur Paul C. Brunson assures us that the surest ways to achieve seven figure success is by simply solving a problem for a million people. Jim McCann did just that when he purchased a $10,000 flower shop in New York

City and incorporated the 1-800-FLOWERS phone number, making it extremely easy to order and send flowers to the ones we love. This simple innovative idea didn't just solve a problem by making it easy to arrange beautiful floral arrangements but it provided one simple solution—convenience. Which is why McCann and his company have managed to report $1.12 billion in 2015 alone per their annual revenue report.

But to be a millionaire you must be willing to put in the work. You must also be willing to live below your means. This means no more eating out every night, no more overspending, no more buying overpriced designer clothes and shoes, and no more unnecessary expenses that destroy your budget. Laying off your morning cup of coffee alone can save you an average of $760 a year, or deciding to cut off your cable TV can save you anywhere from $960-$1,440 annually.

To become a millionaire in today's economy, you have to focus on increasing your income in steady increments to give your funds the necessary lift they need. Another rule of thumb is to save, save, save—save until it hurts and you'll save yourself from being broke.

Saving $100 for 25 years will give you a $30,000 nest egg to fall back on. But by managing to invest $4,830 annually at the age of 25, with an annual return of 7% (after fees) will help you reach millionaire status by age 65.

Lastly, learn to leave the plastic at home and refrain from using credit cards if you can. This basic habit will pay dividends in due time. Warren Buffet said it best. "Someone is sitting in the shade today because someone planted a tree a long time ago."

Therefore, think of planting a seed as saving, and watering the seed as investing, and the shade from the seed that it will provide one day is what it will yield, and the fruit it will produce will be the proof of all your hard work and labor finally paying off. So by working diligently and consistently towards your goal today, your efforts will eventually pay off in the future.

LET SUCCESS INVADE THE CORNERS OF YOUR MIND

Read everything you can find on success and successful people. It's no secret that reading can help boost your intelligence, and aids in the accumulation of information that can be used to your advantage. Reading is also good for the brain since it is neurobiologically demanding on the central nervous system, compared to processing a series of images. So when you allow success to invade the corners of your mind, your mind becomes cornered by success. Have you ever wondered why some of the world's most successful leaders possess some of the same traits? Well, it turns out that most of them read similar literature.

So if you want to be a success, you have to study success, and create a life centered on what you feel the most passionate about. Motivational speaker Eric Thomas adds to this, "When you want to succeed as bad as you want to breathe, then you will be successful." Furthermore, you must get in the habit of pursuing your goals with ambition and intensity. Listen to motivational seminars to help optimize your work ethic. Feed on current events such as business and financial news. Learn as much as you can about the world around you including the ongoing economic issues that plague our country, follow the political decisions being made that affect our lives on a local, national and sometimes international scale. When you make it a habit to do these things it not only helps to keep you informed, but it can be very useful for you as a business owner, especially during tough economic times.

Financial journalist, editor and author B.C. Forbes was obsessed with success. His gift for clear, insightful coverage on the wonderful world of business earned him a following and led to a job offer by a London newspaper. Forbes was very informative, and in sync with the world of commerce. He composed countless articles on business, finance and the thrilling pursuit of entrepreneurship. His passion for economic development was undeniable so in 1942 he started his own magazine with partner Walter Drey, called *Forbes* magazine. Now a global media giant, *Forbes* magazine puts the spotlight on some of the world's wealthiest public figures, from Bill Gates, to Steve Jobs, Warren Buffet, Mark Zuckerberg, Phil Knight, Jeff Bezos, Carlos Slim, Michael Dell, Charles Schwab, Dr. Dre, Sean "Puffy" Combs, and Jay-Z, just to name a few.

Today, Steven Forbes, Jr., (the son of longtime Forbes publisher Malcolm Forbes, who was the grandson of B.C. Forbes) is currently worth $430 million—all because his grandfather allowed success to invade the corners of his mind—and so should you. Now is the time to start thinking of your future and the lifestyle you desire to live. Think of what you've already accomplished, what you want to accomplish and how you're going to accomplish it. Because each day is a new day to be conquered regardless of how many times you've been defeated. So stay focused and achieve your goals one step at a time while granting access to success to invade the corners of your mind.

WHAT DO YOU WANT TO ACCOMPLISH?

As we all know, life is what you make of it, so if it hands you lemons you have the option to make lemonade, lemon cake or lemon water—the choice is yours. Businessman Billy Joe "Red" McCombs is the poster child for accomplishments and what you can make of your life. He opened his first auto dealership at 25 years of age, and at his peak he owned a total of 55 dealerships.

He was also the owner of Clear Channel Communications, now known as iHeartMedia, which owns, operates, programs, and sells airtime for over 1,200 radio stations. McCombs was also the owner of the San Antonio Spurs, the Denver Nuggets, and the Minnesota Vikings at different times of his life. He also got involved with cattle breeding, oil drilling, condo construction, and investing in privately owned companies. McCombs has also financially backed the $25 million private aircraft terminal at Austin-Bergstrom International Airport promising upscale services for private aircraft customers.

Today, McCombs net worth sits at an estimated $1.3 billion because he chose to make lemonade, lemon cake, and lemon water with the lemons life gave him. He's a great example that you can do anything you set your mind to. He didn't allow anything or anyone to hold him back from being successful, and nor should you.

The secret to getting from where you are to where you want to be is working towards your goals before you end up where you *don't* want to be. Begin by documenting your goals because this increases the odds of you actually achieving them. Then commit to them, because people who don't write down their goals and commit to them tend to fail easier than the ones who do. I've also learned that when you can read what you want to achieve, your faith waters the seed for you to believe, until each of your goals are achieved.

So make some time in a place of solitude to focus on what you want out of life—uninterrupted. Identify what your aspirations are and how you plan to accomplish them. Your vision becomes clearer when you do this, as it helps to prepare you to carry out your plans before you actually plan to act. It's almost like seeing your ambitions look back at you, because writing down what you want to achieve will reinforce what you want to receive.

So put some serious thought into what you want to accomplish and give yourself a deadline to finish it. Just make sure that you're setting realistic goals with realistic deadlines. It doesn't work if you write, "I want to lose 20 pounds in 20 hours," because that's impossible. But if you wrote, "I want to lose 20 pounds by November 2018" it now incorporates a measurable outcome, sharpens your focus and adds clarity. So write out a plan of action on how you will complete each of your goals and make progress until it's accomplished.

MAKE PROGRESS UNTIL IT'S ACCOMPLISHED

A masterpiece is the result of many different brush strokes that contribute to the finished painting. Therefore, a picture cannot exist if the individual lines that form a sketch are not drawn to outline it, even a journey of a thousand miles begins with a single step. Because taking action puts you one step closer to your goals instead of continuing to just talking about it.

Just ask modern caveman Angelo Mastropietro, who transformed a 250 million year old cave into a luxurious living pad in Wyre Forest, Worcestershire. He spent approximately 1,000 hours breaking, cutting and carving through rock. He even excavated 70 tons of rubble by hand. With his high level of determination Mastropietro was able to turn his dream into a reality. After eight long months of laboring day and night, Mastropietro's rocky underground home was born. His stylish cave has Wi-Fi capabilities, running water, electricity, a ventilation channel through the floor, a cozy fireplace, a spacious terrace, a dining area, a kitchen, and a bathroom. He also graced it with an extravagant stone shower.

Mastropietro describes building his cave home as an inspiring chapter of his life since it was designed to help cater to his multiple sclerosis and to assist him with transforming his unhealthy lifestyle as a businessman. He says, "The work was a labor of love and I was determined to transform this forgotten cave into something special...and I think we can safely say it will outlive many of the new homes being built today!"

Your achievements are a reflection of your persistence and Mastropietro proves this. The things he completed in this challenging project are a great demonstration that you can't move towards a goal without gaining a clear picture of what you want to accomplish. So you shouldn't just say, "I want a house," or "I want a business." Instead, be more specific and say, "I want to start my own auto detailing business in the next three to six months," or "I want to buy a 3,000 square foot house in Los Angeles by October of next year." Then begin to act on it and make progress until your goal is accomplished.

It never ceases to amaze me how when someone really wants to do something they will always find a way to get it done, but those who don't will always find an excuse. This is why I admire entrepreneurs so much, because one thing we all have in common is our burning desire to make all of our ideas come to life and we know that unless we start *somewhere* we won't get *anywhere*.

BELIEVE IN YOURSELF OR STARVE

Not everyone desires to be a millionaire, or is driven to make money and that's ok, however this still does not expel you from connecting with your purpose. Because the further you drift from it the greater the struggle of life becomes because you exist for a reason. Which is why I'll never drift from being an entrepreneur, photographer, graphic designer, business coach, author and songwriter.

Furthermore, there are many reasons to start and run your own business, but the rewards of small-business ownership do not come overnight. It takes determination, patience, persistence, consistency, and the will to make sacrifices. Iconic entrepreneur Rowland Macy is the perfect example of what it takes to truly flourish in managing an enterprise. With his determination constantly being put to the test Macy accumulated a portfolio of failures, but he never gave up and good thing he didn't. Because who knew that one day his small fancy dry goods store on the famous corner of 14th Street and 6th Avenue in New York City would grow to be one of America's largest retail chains with over 800 locations across the U.S.

Today, Macy's operates out of 45 states and has experienced tremendous growth since its grand opening in 1858, when Macy only generated $11.06 in sales his first day in business. However, Macy didn't get discouraged, and it's a good thing he didn't, because by the end of the year he managed to gross over $80,000 in total sales—not bad for a successful failure who didn't fail to succeed.

Over time, Macy expanded his operation and occupied 11 more buildings and eventually began to sell many different categories of merchandise. By 1997, there were hundreds of Macy's stores across 37 states and the company quickly followed up with the launch of Macys.com. The website helped to broaden their reach in the online market and ultimately ignited more sales.

Today, Macy's is worth over $23 billion dollars, and every year more than 20 million shoppers visit Macy's on 34th street in New York's Herald Square. Macy's is also known for its highly animated Thanksgiving Day parade. Each year more than 3.5 million spectators line up along the route to watch the oversized balloon characters, marching bands, floats, and a host of celebrities. In addition, the parade draws in an additional 50 million television viewers who watch it live on NBC.

But it wasn't always like this for Macy because before he passed away in 1877, he failed at his four previous attempts at retail. He even went bankrupt in the process. He worked in his father's shop for several years before opening his own needle and thread store in 1844, in Boston, Massachusetts, before it failed. Macy then tried selling dry goods in 1846, but this store also failed. He then worked briefly in his brother-in-law's shop in Boston, but that didn't work out either. So in 1849 he fled to California, anxious to dive into the gold rush. But unfortunately he didn't find what he was looking for—gold. After failing at finding wealth out west, Macy returned to Massachusetts and opened a dry goods store again in 1851, with his brother. They saw modest success, but not enough for Macy to stay. So in 1858 he left Massachusetts and opened a small store in a low-rent neighborhood in New York City's Herald Square—and the rest became history.

The point is, never give up. Instead, get back up and get going again. Yes, it hurts when failure beats us up, but why allow yourself to feel stress when you can rip failure apart with success? Believe in yourself, and be brave, or fear will make you its slave. Did you know that the most common trait successful entrepreneurs share is their confidence? And in this world you must have confidence in your abilities to create endless possibilities in a world full of stress, worry and negativity. Steve Jobs refused to tolerate people who didn't believe in themselves because he knew that confidence is contagious and he wanted everyone on his team to catch it and spread it.

THE POWER OF PATIENCE

Some people know where they want to be in life, but most refuse to go through the process in order to get there. However, patience and persistence are an unbeatable combination to help get you going. Professional boxers, for example, know they have to be patient and persistent before deciding when, where and how to strike their opponent, because they know in order to win it's all about **timing and accuracy**. Sometimes the strongest, fastest and most skillful boxers in the world lose fights because of their lack of patience when, in fact, this is one of the most critical components to winning the fight.

A boxer who is patient, and who can stay on his feet long enough for his opponent to use up all of his strength until he's physically and mentally exhausted, will most likely come out on top because of his ability to be patient while he's inside the ring.

Another great example of patience requires us to turn our attention to two-time Superbowl winner Peyton Manning who had over 500 touchdown passes before he retired. This is the most touchdown passess in an NFL career to date. But he would have failed to accomplish this if he hadn't practiced patience under pressure. He knew that if he wanted to be successful at carrying out various plays he'd have to tolerate delay when a play didn't go his way. Aware of this, Manning knew that he had to remain emotionally stable through the duration of the game and endure any displeasure he may have had toward himself or his teammates when obstacles got in the way.

Since patience is the condition of one's endurance under difficult circumstances your actions will condition you to either fail or succeed. So your ability to remain disciplined when confronted with setbacks and unforeseen problems will reveal the true quality of your mental toughness. So if you learn to grow your patience you'll also learn to grow your success. Patience can be bitter, but its fruit can be sweet. It took producers and managers eight months to prepare for a 12- day shoot in New York City for the movie The Dark Knight Rises. That's more than half the year, 243 days to be exact, just to capture a 12-day shoot on film. "It was a very daunting task, but it actually went very smoothly," said director Christopher Nolan.

Yes, waiting for a goal or a dream to materialize can be agonizing. But it takes patience, persistence and endurance to reach it. Nothing great is ever accomplished without these three qualities. Therefore, it would benefit us if we began viewing patience as a muscle that we must exercise daily! For example, if someone's driving below the speed limit and they're in front of you, this becomes the perfect time to exercise patience. As you feel your blood begin to boil and your emotions begin to rage practice gaining control over your temper, breathe slowly, and relax. You should soon feel your anger beginning to fade.

If you apply this technique any time you feel annoyed, frustrated or infuriated it will help you to keep calm simply because in doing so you're not losing self-control, but rather gaining it. As a result, you'll keep yourself balanced and level-headed because those who practice self-control cannot be overpowered by things that are outside of their control.

It's a natural emotion to feel upset when our needs aren't being met. But it doesn't mean that we have to turn into the Incredible Hulk any time that people let us down. So do the best you can do, with what you can do, because you can't do anything about what you can't do. You can't do anything about walking into an important meeting late, but what you can do is try to be on time next time. This is what having patience is all about. Learn to stay mentally calm and master accepting the things you cannot change.

THE POWER OF WORDS

Not only do words have power, they are power. The words we speak are so powerful that they can send a nation to war, start a revolution, destroy relationships, and ignite change. Words have this amazing power to lift us up as well as bring us down, they have the ability to transform how we feel, how we think, and how we live our lives. Unfortunately, most people will never realize just how powerful words truly are, as they carry the strength to heal, and at the same time can influence people to kill. The wrong choice of words can be cancerous to a person's soul but the right group of words can nourish it.

The words we use are individual expressions of thought conveyed through written or verbal means of communication. So when thoughts are expressed, the right choice of words can make all the difference. Since words are units of language that embody meaning, practicing to think before we speak can actually help us speak more effectively. So the next time you find yourself being tempted to make a negative remark remember that words mark the heart and stain the consciousness. This is why it's essential to learn the language of positivity, because speaking positively and being positive can have a positive influence on your life.

It has been said that the average human being has anywhere between 50,000-70,000 thoughts each day. If this holds true, this means we have roughly 35-48 thoughts per minute. So what if we took 10% of our thoughts and converted them into positive words of affirmation? Words of affirmation are encouraging statements with positive energy attached to them.

For example, imagine that you wake up each day and simply say, "Today will be an extraordinary day packed with extraordinary opportunities." This will not only help jumpstart your morale, it will also help to establish a positive wave of energy into your day, before your day establishes a negative wave of energy in you. However, not all affirmations are created equal because different affirmations help you get to different destinations.

For instance, if I were to say, "I will start making positive choices in my life," then this will help recondition my mind to make better choices; but if I were to say, "Having money makes me evil," then I jeopardize my financial stability. There's no debate that affirmations help to strengthen our way of thinking, due to the choice in thoughts we choose to think.

Furthermore, when we openly declare our hopes, dreams and aspirations for our future our confidence drives our desires into manifestation. Words are empowering, and positive words of affirmation bring empowerment. In addition, when these uplifting words seep into our conscious and subconscious mind we ultimately inspire ourselves to succeed and we are instantly motivated to live up to our highest potential. But most importantly, affirmations inspire us to speak the change we desire to see, until we see the change we decided to speak. With this in view, here are 11 powerful affirmations that will help you on your quest to success.

So practice speaking them into your life until your life reveals what you spoke.

1. I have a purpose and my purpose has me.

2. I am ready to take my life to the next level and today I will.

3. Each day I will become more successful than I was yesterday.

4. As long as I keep believing, I will keep achieving.

5. I will commit to my goals.

6. I will always reside in a prosperous state of mind.

7. I will defend myself from all negativity with the shield of positivity.

8. Today is the day I will act on my dreams.

9. I am a demonstration of excellence because I am destined to excel.

10. My confidence will reign and I shall reign in confidence.

11. I will always use the divine power of my mind to manifest the things I desire in real time.

If you're anything like me and believe that *you are what you think*, then we are in unison with the fact that life truly stems from our thoughts. Therefore, we must practice translating our thoughts into words and eventually into actions if we want to see an everlasting change in our lives.

THE POWER OF BELIEF

Your perception is the foundation of how you think, and on this foundation your beliefs are built. So when things happen to you, remember that it's not how they happen, it's what *you think* about what happened and how well *you respond* to it. The truth is, many things are a result of perception. Your love life depends on someone's perception of you; the decision to hire you was based on your qualifications, but mainly on someone else's perception of you.

Your influence as a parent and the impact you have on your kids is based on your kids' overall perception of you as their mother or father. Our perceptions enforce our way of thinking, and our way of thinking enforces what we believe. Do you think if William Washington Browne who was a former slave, had not believed in himself that he would have become the first African-American to open a bank in 1889?

This just re-affirms once again that our beliefs affect every area of our lives from our mood, relationships, career, success, wealth, well-being, and religious preference. The Greek philosopher Epictetus once said that "Men are disturbed not by events, but by the views which they take of them." In other words, it's not the *events* we experience that disturb us; it's our *interpretation* of them that do. Our interpretation of everything we endure determines how much those experiences mean to us, which ultimately triggers how much they affect us.

This is a poignant example of how we all perceive the world through our own eyes, and with our own lens. Therefore, it is our views that color in our perceptions. So if you believe the world is infested with evil, then you will live life believing that evil has infested the world. As a result, your beliefs about the world will influence how you respond to the world, and how you respond to the world will reflect your view of the world, because your view of the world is ultimately the reality of your worldview. For this reason, we must carefully and accurately monitor our cognitive belief systems since our thoughts are what drive our behaviors.

Moreover, do you know how Brian Shaw became recognized as the strongest man in the world? Simple, he *believed* that he was, therefore he trained and became what he believed. Standing at 6'8" and weighing almost 440 pounds, Shaw currently holds two World's Strongest Man competition titles and can bench press over 600 pounds of weight; his squat max is 800 pounds, and he can deadlift 1140 pounds, all due to his amazing size and strength and the power that comes from him believing in himself.

He also finished in 4th place in the 2012 American Spirit Championship after detaching his bicep. Shaw says, "Other guys would quit almost immediately, not me, I did the rest of the contest with my bicep torn off." He accomplished this simply because he *believed* that he could, so he did. The point is, you can do anything you want in life if you believe in it enough. The more you understand the power of belief, the more **confident you'll** become that you can achieve what you perceive—but only if you truly believe. As we become more aware of ourselves and the world we live in, we learn that the structure of our belief systems evolve from our own theories, knowledge, and convictions that we possess as human beings.

This plays an intricate role in shaping our world view of the material world because our belief systems are the building blocks of our thoughts. For instance, if I believe that I'm an amazing songwriter (without any positive knowledge of this being true), my mental acceptance of this proposition becomes embedded into my cognitive belief system. The power of this belief will then express itself through my behavior because my behavior is directed by my thoughts, and so are my actions. We create what we think; therefore, the thoughts we choose to believe become the architects of our reality.

So if I believe I'm a failure, my reality is going to conform to my mentality. You are what you believe, because you believe that is what you are. But if you decide to reprogram your way of thinking and begin believing that you are a true magnet for success, your reformed mentality will reinforce these new, positive ways of thinking into your reality.

Beliefs are so powerful that it's not uncommon for people to openly accept a belief as true without any evidence to back their belief. Since 80 percent of what we learn is through our eyes, what we believe is often based on what we see. For instance, if you see a woman with tears in her eyes you may believe that her tears are a sign of heartbreak, or sadness, and you'd probably feel compelled to ask her if she's ok.

However, if you believe that her tears are tears of joy it extinguishes your concern. See how your perceptions govern your beliefs? This is because your personal perception of reality is based on the personal beliefs you hold in the womb of your mentality. However, this does not necessarily make your beliefs real, except for the fact that you make them real and you making them real is what forms "your" reality in "your" mind. So remember that you can have anything you want, as long as you're willing to give up the belief that you can't have it.

THE POWER INSIDE YOU

From the moment you came out of your mother's womb you possessed great skill, power, and strength. These attributes were sown into the physical properties of your kinetic energy and as a result you were chosen to carry out an assignment here on earth. Since each day is a gift that you're presented with, you must use your gifts in the present.

So, if you're on the wrong path, take hold of your courage and make the changes that are needed in your life. This will ultimately bring you satisfaction, because your gift is your power. In fact, your gift has the ability to produce an effect, and anything that can produce an effect can cause a series of events that can ultimately transform the world. The truth is, you have an amazing skill inside of you, a special intelligence, a unique strength, and a talent that wants, needs, and yearns to be expressed.

However, if you imprison these talents that you were born with, you prevent others from receiving the true benefit of your purpose. A real-life demonstration of a gift and its power came into this world on January 29, 1954 in the small 7.5 square mile town of Kosciusko, Mississippi. Born into poverty but destined for greatness, she would one day show the world that it's not your circumstances, but your heart that determines how far you go in life. Growing up, kids would tease her for wearing dresses made from potato sacks, not realizing who stood before them and that one day she would be the world's first African-American female billionaire. She would also have her own personal stylist who would help her select her wardrobe for her own TV show and eventually for her own network.

But before achieving fortune and fame she endured traumatic childhood experiences, being brutally raped at the tender age of 9, constant episodes of sexual molestation between the ages of 10 and 14, and a history of physical abuse. But still her gift and its power helped her rise above her childhood trauma. The attempts to despoil her soul did not prevail because she wasn't knitted into existence to become someone's object, but rather, she was chosen by an almighty force who had already established her worth from birth.

She was destined to prosper in the world's system of financial slavery. She even endured the cataclysm of both racial and gender discrimination in the world of American broadcasting in the 1980's. But Oprah Gail Winfrey didn't allow this to get in her way. She still managed to overpower the adversity and tragedy that tried to destroy her life. Her tenacious ability to push through these awful events demonstrates the core of her resilience.

Oprah once explained that these experiences that she suffered as a child inspired her need to empathize with people in her daily life. As a result, her list of accomplishments have only continued to grow as she is best known for hosting her own TV talk show the *Oprah Winfrey show* from 1986 to 2011 completing over 4,500 episodes before its end. She is also an actress, philanthropist, publisher and producer and has even managed to open up a Leadership Academy for Girls in South Africa, with the goal of helping to support the development of a new generation of dynamic women leaders.

In addition, many stars have shot to fame thanks to Oprah from Iyanla Vanzant, Dr. Phil, Dr. Oz, Suze Orman and celebrity cook Rachael Ray just to name a few. Moreover, Oprah first made her film debut in *The Color Purple*, directed by Steven Spielberg, which was nominated for 11 Academy Awards. She even launched her own magazine, titled *O* magazine in 2000, and has graced the front cover of every issue. In 2011 she launched OWN: The Oprah Winfrey Network, the first and only network named for, and inspired by, a single iconic leader. She has made countless contributions to charity and started her own foundation in 1998 called The Angel Network, which was established to encourage people from around the world to make a difference in the lives of others.

Lastly, as of the publication of this book, Oprah has inhabited the earth for over 22,645 days and has made each and every one of them count towards her purpose.

Her ignited desire to use her gift for good has allowed her to triumph over some of life's biggest obstacles and hurdles despite having to face new challenges each day. There is no debate that she is intellectually equipped to deal with success and the demands that come with your purpose. She says, "You are built not to shrink down to less but to blossom into more...the right to choose your own path is a sacred privilege. Use it."

DEFEAT SELF-DEFEATING THOUGHTS

The same picture in a different frame can look very different, because of the different frame. Likewise, learning how to reframe your thoughts can help how you perceive different events and situations that occur in your life. For example, a negative experience can have a positive effect if you allow it to, by simply learning and growing from it. The event itself does not change; however, your interpretation of it can. So learning how to reframe your way of thinking can help you frame new positive ways of thinking. Because both positivity and negativity come from the same place—our thoughts.

For this reason, we should always be aware of what we tell ourselves and, more importantly, what we "think" of ourselves. As human beings we're always trying to make sense of the things we live through by analyzing the events around us, and cast strong judgment on what we could've done better. But sometimes, when we're faced with challenges and obstacles they can turn our internal voice into a negative one. This is when we must learn how to silence our inner critic by replacing false beliefs with factual ones.

For instance, if I were to think or say things like, "No one will ever read my book," or "I'll never become a best-selling author," this way of thinking will ultimately stunt my success as a writer. It will not help get me very far as an author because thinking in this fashion will only decorate my mind with self-defeating thoughts that will ultimately lead to self-defeating behavior.

Gary Zukov, author of *Seat of the Soul*, said it best. "By choosing your thoughts, and selecting which emotional currents you will release and which ones you will reinforce, will determine the quality of your light." This is because our thoughts are so powerful that they have the power to affect our day, business, work ethic, relationships, purpose, and, most importantly, our lives as a whole, because negative thoughts drag away positive ones. So besides some of your closest friends and family being dream killers, you can be your own dream killer. When you tell yourself things like, "I can't do it," or "I'm not good enough," you bury yourself in doubt and the casket begins to close on your dreams. But if your thoughts can change, your life can change with it. So instead of feeding self-defeating thoughts with thoughts of defeat, reframe your way of thinking, and digest thoughts of what you can become.

Just imagine if billionaire Nick Woodman had accepted defeat after failing miserably with two online start-ups. He would have never received accolades for his tremendous business success. His first start-up that failed was a cheap electronics business with just a $2 mark-up on every gadget he sold, this was quickly shut down; and the other start-up was FunBug, an online marketing company, in which he managed to raise $3.9 million in venture capital funding. But a year later, in 2001, Woodman lost all of his investors' money and had to shut his business down, once again.

After losing close to $4 million in start-up cash, Nick was forced to look failure in the eye once more, but his thoughts did not allow him to accept defeat as his fate. So, in 2002, Nick was so committed to being successful that he began working on a camera that would revolutionize videography forever. He discovered capturing various activities in a cool new way. When he founded GoPro he said, "I was so afraid that GoPro was going to go away like Funbug that I would work my ass off."

As a result, Woodman is now among the youngest self-made billionaires of the 1,426 individuals on the billionaire list. With a current estimated net worth of $2.3 billion, Nick proved that he was determined to prevail, and he refused to be engulfed by self-defeating thoughts. He didn't allow failure to stand in his way; instead, his failures helped him to find his way. Refusing to be kidnapped by doubt, Nick deliberately used his faith to sustain him until his dreams became real. So don't let self-defeating thoughts plague your mind. Instead, take control over your life by fixing your brilliance upon your strengths in order to define your future in the present.

Buy a journal and write out the things that are hindering you from chasing your dreams. Then, write down everything you can do to make them come true. As you do this, remind yourself that you are an intelligent human being with remarkable mental strength and the ability to do great things with every breath your life brings.

FIGHT FOR YOUR DREAMS

You have to fight for your dreams or your dreams will fight with you. There is nothing more upsetting than laboring for another man's dream while disregarding yours. It's been said that 97% of people who quit chasing their dreams are hired by the 3% who didn't. So why be an employee, in exchange for pay, when you have the ability to be your own boss and determine how much you deserve to get paid?

Although, I am not completely against having a job, because some people just don't have an entrepreneur mindset and that's ok. Then there are those who just absolutely love their jobs and are content with what they do and that's ok as well. However, I am against anyone who gives up on their dreams just because someone is willing to pay them weekly or bi-weekly to labor for theirs. In other words, if you know you have an entrepreneur mind and you have what it takes to operate your own business and determine your own salary, then why stay in a position working for someone else who's putting a cap on your a salary? This is an ultimate violation to your purpose because when you suppress your dreams, you subdue your ambitions and jeopardize the importance of your existence.

Malcom Forbes once said "The biggest mistake people make in life is not trying to make a living at what they enjoy." Moreover, you have everything it takes to achieve your inner ambitions and the intelligence to live the life you feel worthy of. Did you know that over 70% of working professionals hate their job? Simply because they've been hired to carry out certain tasks and duties that they often have absolutely no passion for. In most cases, they get trained for a job that eventually paralyzes their emotions because it's basically a job that will never fulfill them.

I also understand the desire of wanting to be your own boss but being afraid to leave the security of a paycheck. This is something many people struggle with, and more than often they simply can't afford to because they have too many bills to pay. So they settle for a career working 40 hours a week—sometimes more—building up their employer's dreams, all while losing time to begin building theirs.

But if you have a dream, you have to fight for it. To fight means to attack and defend. Therefore, if you want to be a doctor you must attack self-defeating thoughts with thoughts of being undefeated, and defend your dreams of being a doctor from every dream-killing enemy.

Be fearless. As a serial achiever in the making, you have to constantly train to defeat your toughest opponent—and that opponent is you! So make it your duty to win the war inside your head because you are your own worst critic when you're trying to accomplish a goal.

It's time to outwork your doubts and surpass your fears. Cease fighting *with* your ideas, and start fighting *for* them. Prepare to be victorious and keep fighting to be whatever it is you aspire to be. Whether your ambition is to be a lawyer, doctor, author, actor, musician, chef, producer, engineer, screenwriter, dancer, model, photographer, personal trainer, professional athlete, or entrepreneur, fight until you can't fight anymore.

Undefeated boxing champion Floyd Mayweather once said, "It can be tough chasing a goal that's so far into the future—or in many cases, completely undefined. But if you feel a constant pressure, and if you can imagine what will happen if you fall behind, you'll be more motivated to push."

PUSH

Life is no walk in the park and at times it absolutely sucks. But you still have to push until something happens. So push when you're strong, and push when you're weak. Push for your purpose and what you aspire to be. If you never had support from your mother or father, push harder! Push to go far, but once you get there, push to go farther. Push for your success, push when you're at your lowest and push when you're at your best. Push for financial freedom and push to get out of debt. Push through your troubles, and push through your stress. Push for your future, and when your ambition is put to the test.

Push, push, push some more. Push until you can't push anymore. Push through your fear of being an entrepreneur. Push when you take a loss. Push to be your own boss. Push with your mind, and push it with force. Push for the life you deserve to live, push for your family, and most importantly, push for your kids. Push for yourself, and push for your health, push for your dreams and push for your wealth. Push through the sun and push through the rain, push through the storm and push through the pain. No matter what, never stop pushing, and always allow motivation to push through your veins. PUSH!

TAKING FINANCIAL RISKS

All investments carry risk, but not all investments return a reward. For this reason, it's always best to decide if it's worth the risk and if you can afford to lose your investment if it doesn't generate a return. But no matter how you look at it everything in life is a risk. Nothing is guaranteed. Getting into your car and driving to work every day is a risk. Especially when you consider that there are over 35,000 motor vehicle deaths annually in the U.S. alone. For many, taking a risk is a scary thing because the fog of uncertainty is always there.

But if you decide to not take a risk today, you risk missing out on what you can become tomorrow. For example, if Richard and Maurice McDonald had never taken a chance to revolutionize the fast-food

The Art of Believing & Achieving

industry, then the McDonald's franchise would have never become the world's largest chain of fast food hamburgers, serving over 65 million customers daily in 119 countries across the globe. Today, McDonald's is worth over $90 billion and it's still growing worldwide.

Therefore, taking risks is about taking chances, and sometimes these chances can make you very successful or very unsuccessful. That's the nature of the game. This is why it's so important to practice risk management. In a world full of uncertainty, when you are trying to assess probability, risk management can help you identify, analyze and alleviate guesswork before you invest.

For instance, let's say you're interested in buying a business or investing in one. You should always ask to review the company's financial statements before you move forward. This will help you to identify the level of risk involved. There are also environmental risks you must consider. Ask about the company's demographic data in order to help identify their key customers and the median household income in the surrounding area. Because you may not benefit much by buying a business in the middle of a desert.

Do some research and see if there is a demand for what the company is selling in that particular area. Carrying out these simple steps, and more, can possibly save you from taking a loss on your investment, and can help you to generate a well-earned return.

In essence, risk management has so many benefits because it helps to manage many different factors that may interfere with a business achieving its goal. It assesses the potential outcome of an investment and can help you determine if there is any room for economic gain. Scaling risk also helps you to carry out the appropriate series of actions or inactions in your decision to invest or not. Although we cannot avoid risk entirely, we should do our very best to eliminate our exposure to taking a total loss by taking out the necessary time to perform research.

MONEY MANAGEMENT

Do you find yourself living from paycheck to paycheck? Are you always strapped for cash? Do you often wonder where all your money went just days after you got paid? Or maybe you make a lot of money but it rarely makes it into your savings account. If this sounds like you, maybe it's time to create a budget to help you with your financial goals, because your budget is your best friend. So as we discuss some of the key principles of money management, I want you to see how budgeting can enhance your life.

Did you know that as your life evolves so should your finances? But if you show a lack of financial discipline towards your savings, investment portfolio, and retirement fund then you put yourself at risk of not having anything to fall back on once you retire or incase face an economic hardship. For this reason, learning how to manage your finances wisely is extremely important because it can help you manage your living expenses. It can also help you to refrain from purchasing items that add no significant value to your overall standard of living. In fact, keeping track of your expenses is the first step towards your financial independence.

The next series of steps should involve you analyzing your living expenses, monitoring your income, managing your consumer debt, then establishing a budget and sticking to it. Performing these four task alone can help give your finances a boost. This approach also helps you to keep track of your spending, debt to income ratio, and the inflow/outflow of your money.

So before you go and blow your check at the mall, on things with little to no value, always remind yourself of your financial goals and why it's important to stay committed to them. When you learn to spend less than what you earn, you'll earn more than what you spend, and that's how you win. Practicing this helps to strengthen the structure of your financial foundation and is a reflection of your discipline. However, if your finances continue to go unregulated you will always struggle with money management, whether you make $10,000, $50,000 or $100,000 a year. This is why you must budget to save, and save to invest. But this cannot be accomplished without keeping track of your funds. The best way to keep tabs on how much money actually comes in and out of your hands on a daily, weekly, monthly, and yearly basis is as follows:

1. Income vs. Expenses
Base your income and expenses on reality. If you can't truly afford the rent for that new apartment, or the mortgage for the house that you want, or the note for the car that you want, then don't buy it. Live within your means, by all means.

2. Keep a Log
Record your expenses. Write out your fixed vs. variable expenses. Your rent, for example, is considered a fixed monthly expense whereas your electric bill will vary.

3. Consume Less

Stop being wasteful. Turn off all lights, appliances and electronics when not in use. Stop leaving your TV on all night, and your computer running. Instead, make it a habit to unplug any and all items when not being utilized. Learning to turn off your water heater alone when not in use can save you up to $30-40 a month on your energy bill.

4. Needs vs. Wants

Ask yourself, "do I need it?" Because you don't *need* those $250 pair of Air Jordan's, you *want* those $300 pair of Air Jordan's. And ladies, you also don't *need* those $945 Christian Louboutin red bottom shoes, you *want* those $945 Christian Louboutin red bottom shoes. See the difference?

5. Divide Into Shares

Practice allocating 20% of your income towards your financial priorities. Focus on building up your savings, retirement, and emergency funds, while paying down your debt in the process. So for instance, let's say you make $35,000 a year. You should set aside at least $4,800 for your financial priorities.

6. Have Fun
Save for a vacation. Sometimes we get so caught up in work, work, work that we don't make time to play. So save for your dream getaway and make time to have some fun in the sun.

Lastly, eat out less. This one by far was the hardest one for me personally, and still is, because I love to eat. However, the cost of eating out daily adds up rather quickly. Let's say you eat out twice a day, for breakfast and lunch, and each meal costs $9.99 plus tax, which is normally 8.25 percent. That gives you a total of $10.81 that you would spend on each meal, giving you a grand total of $21.62 that you would spend on two meals daily.

If you did this for a month straight you would spend $648.60 on eating out twice a day, and $7,783.20 if you did this for a year straight. That's about the cost of a used vehicle. Furthermore, sometimes we fail to understand the importance of spending money sensibly and saving it so that it can be utilized in more efficient ways. This is why budgeting is so important because if we are poor managers of our finances we will fail at other financial temptations that we encounter.

Also, work on eliminating high interest rate credit cards and attempt to double up on the payments if you can afford to. It's no secret that credit card companies make money by collecting interest on the balance owed at the end of each month until the balance is paid in full. In addition, most credit card companies charge annual, over-the-limit, cash-advance, and late payment fees to keep you in debt even longer because it's more money for them.

Also, if you don't have a 401K retirement plan you can start funding an IRA. You can also defer paying income tax on up to $5,500 contributed to an IRA. Another rule of thumb is, in order to meet your retirement needs, experts estimate that you will need at least 70-90 percent of your pre-retirement income to maintain your standard of living once you stop working. So take charge of your financial future by planning ahead. There are many financial advisor companies to choose from that can help you personalize your retirement and investment needs.

INVEST IN YOURSELF

To invest means to put money into something with the hope of gaining a profitable return in the near future. Although this can be a bit intimidating for some people, the truth is that if you don't risk investing in yourself today, then you put your future at risk tomorrow because you my friend, are your most valuable asset. So, why not put your time, energy and money into you?

Start by discovering your inner strengths and the things you're great at, and begin putting those strengths to work. Also, learn to manage your time properly. Avoid spending too much time on social media reading posts and posting selfies of yourself all day. As an entrepreneur in the making you don't have time to waste. So always focus on the task at hand and use your time as effectively as you can. In addition, having a plan and being organized in your daily tasks and duties is a great way to stay on track.

You should also avoid spending countless hours browsing the internet and watching TV instead try reading more. The time you spend indulging in these activities could be time well spent mastering your craft or doing something more productive. Try setting daily, weekly, and monthly goals for yourself. This not only helps you to push yourself but it also helps you to grow your accomplishments. Keep track of all the things you complete and at the end of the year you can look back on how well you achieved your goals.

As you make progress you may want to look into finding a mentor. Although this may be a bit of a challenge finding a mentor can pay off in a lot of ways because they can help you find career success. They are known to be positive, yet highly motivated people who can help you find the lessons in your life experiences and help you to use those lessons to your advantage.

Lastly, never be afraid to invest in yourself financially. Believe it or not, you have the ability to design the kind of life you want but you have to make smart decisions and spend your time, energy and money wisely. This will ultimately help you get what you want out of life, instead of wasting your time on things you have no desire for.

KEEP YOUR CREDIT HEALTHY

If you ever plan on getting approved for a credit card, mortgage loan, business loan, personal loan, or a personal line of credit you will have to maintain a healthy credit score. Also known as your FICO score, this score helps lenders to determine if you're a high risk borrower. So the higher your score the less risky you appear to the lender. Once you develop a clear understanding of what affects your score you can take all the necessary measures to improve it. Below are the five metrics that determine your credit rating, they are as follows:

1. Payment history
2. Current loans and credit card debt

3. The length of your credit history
4. Types of credit
5. Shopping for new credit

As a borrower, your credit score also determines the interest rate you'll be charged on your loans and credit cards. This is why it's important to make sure that accurate information is being reported on your credit report each month. The Fair Credit Reporting Act (FCRA) requires all three credit reporting companies—Equifax, Experian, and TransUnion—to provide you with a free copy of your credit report, at your request, once every 12 months. You can do this by logging on to annualcreditreport.com. Nearly 80 percent of all credit reports contain inaccuracies or erroneous accounts. Therefore, a thorough analysis of your credit profile should become a monthly priority.

Once you have analyzed your report, if you believe that inaccurate information has been reported there are a countless number of credit repair agencies that will help you fix these errors. But be cautious, because a lot of them are rip-offs as an alternative you can learn how to repair, rebuild and protect your credit yourself, for free.

This prevents you from having to pay some so-called credit repair company $100 or more each month with minimal to no changes at all on your credit report. Now here are a few tips to help you maintain a healthy credit score.

1. **Pay on time**

    Avoid allowing your accounts to fall into a delinquent status. You usually have 30-60 days after a bill is due to make a partial payment or a payment in the full amount before it's reported as delinquent.

2. **Don't overspend**

    Try to keep all your balances low on your credit cards and other revolving lines of credit. This will also help keep your debt to income ratio low.

3. **Know the consequences**

Prevent derogatory information from going onto your report because they normally stay on your credit file for 7-10 years. Derogatories are foreclosures, tax liens, bankruptcy filings, accounts in collections, and any civil judgments you may have against you, such as lawsuits.

4. **Put it into one loan**

   Consolidate your debt. Paying off multiple high interest rate credit cards and loans is costly. But consolidating those debts into a personal loan with a 12 percent interest rate for 60 months is better than trying to pay down a $10,000 credit card balance with a 23.24% monthly interest rate.

Following these four simple steps alone help you to improve and maintain a healthy credit score. So make it a habit to manage your debt responsibly, make sure that you're making all of your monthly payments on time.

BUSINESS PARTNERSHIPS

A business partnership with the right person, going in the right direction, can lead the both of you right to success. But a business partnership with the wrong person can be an absolute nightmare. During the summer of 2015 I decided to go into business with a younger gentleman who appeared to be a go-getter like myself. So we decided to become partners and purchase a small 24 hour convenience store with the addition of beer and wine. It was the right size, at the right price, in the right location.

Excited about our new venture, I was ready to turn our store into a cash cow. So after doing some extensive research on how to maximize your revenue operating a convenience store I was ready to get to work. Excited by the wealth of information that I discovered, my creative juices were ready to flow. Little did I know, my partner, on the other hand, had other plans. He expressed his idea to turn our convenience store into a neighborhood lounge with a liquor bar, and a smoothie bar and a deli to serve hot subs. He also wanted it to be a place where kids could come do their homework after school and play video games and have video game tournaments, with women in bikini's standing outside holding up signs with our sub of the day specials. My immediate response was "Are you nuts"!

Keep in mind that at the time I had just learned that he was very limited in capital so most of the shelves would go understocked for weeks. I remember there being a lot of expired potato chips, snacks and beverages. And once we threw it all away the store looked like it had been completely ran sacked! It looked so empty that you would have thought we were going out of business. I had to get used to hearing our customers ask "Are you guys open?" Talk about embarrassing. But it gets worse.

Because the following week he purchased three medium-sized couches and placed them in the center of our store and mounted a TV on the side of the wall without my approval. So once you walked inside the store you saw empty beverage coolers to your left, three black and white pleather couches in the center of the floor, and several half empty candy racks to your right. In total disbelief, I knew my investment was in trouble and that our venture was about to take a turn for the worst, and before I could blink—it did. Because it was soon brought to my attention that my partner had various people staying the night in the back of the store without my knowledge or consent for various reasons.

He also had a habit of giving away our candy, soda and chips (the very little that we did have) for free to our customers whenever he felt like it. After several conversations with him about the direction the store was going in, it wasn't long before we dissolved our partnership due to irreconcilable differences.

So although, I'm very grateful for the lessons that came out of it, I can't help but warn people about the rewards and dangers of a business partnership. Although they are very common, business partnerships can be incredibly hard to sustain because they're like a marriage and if both parties don't see eye to eye it can get tricky. Therefore, it would be in your best interest to learn how to legally structure a business partnership and decide in advance who gets what, and what responsibilities each person has before you put it in black and white. You should also detail in your partnership agreement how you will resolve disagreements, and who owns what percentage of the company, because if one person wants to cut costs by downsizing but the other wants to expand, who has the final say so?

To this day, I wish I had structured our partnership in this fashion because it would have outlined the terms and conditions of the business relationship and would have helped us to resolve conflicts within the business. Opportunities like the one we had only come around every couple of years. But it taught me the importance of working smarter at the right things and the destruction that can come from working so hard at the wrong things. Instead, it's best to focus on creating a business that's valuable. Work on providing things that people need. Identify problems that people share and find a way to solve them. This doesn't take rocket science, nor an MBA to do so.

There's absolutely no reason why you should waste money on things that don't make money. Instead, learn your customer by studying what they buy the most, interact with them, build a rapport with them, resolve any and all issues they may have and make them feel comfortable in the process. Because when you begin working smarter towards the right things you tend to focus less on the wrong things. For instance, you shouldn't try adding a taxi service to a donut shop, when the focus should be the donut shop, and you certainly shouldn't try running a pizza shop inside of a vitamin shop the two just don't mix.

Unfortunately, my partner failed at this and was trying to incorporate too many things into one business, until our business, was out of business. Therefore, there are two lessons that need to be learned. The first is when going into business as partners learn how to legally structure the partnership contractually before going into business with them verbally.

The second is when you're trying to grow a business, one must avoid the temptation to try to do every single thing they can think of to make it a success because this is how you actually fail. Instead, focus on what your business is, what it does and how you can do it better than everyone else who's doing it. Write out what your goals are in detail and what measures you're going to take to accomplish them. This will help you to avoid jumping from idea to idea. Also, always remember that not everyone who runs a business has business sense. Sometimes it just means that at that time, starting a business made sense.

THE ECONOMY'S PULSE

"I hate sales," is what I hear many people say. But the truth is sales is what keeps the pulse of the world's economy palpitating. Today, over 14 million salespeople earn a living by persuading people to purchase the products or services they have for sale. This means that they are steadily trying to convince potential buyers to change their mind, attitude and behavior towards an idea, place or object until they successfully close the sale.

Perhaps this is one of the reasons why self-made billionaire Carlos Slim is currently one of the richest men in the world, with an estimated net worth of $72.9 billion. Slim has not only proven that he is a very savvy investor with a global portfolio of investments in communications, real estate, construction, multiple airlines, media, technology, retail, the restaurant industry, industrial production, and finance, but he has also demonstrated his ability to put together an effective sales team and him being one of the richest men in the world, is a result of this.

If it weren't for sales, Slim's multi-billion dollar enterprise América Movil would not exist and it would not currently have over 289 million mobile customers and more than 21 million television subscribers—and that's just one of his companies.

Furthermore, it is not uncommon to hear about entrepreneurs who fail from a lack of sales. It doesn't matter how passionate you are about your product, if a company struggles to make sales it will struggle to stay in business. Author Brian Tracy says, "Without sales, our entire society would come to a grinding halt. The only real creators of wealth in our society are businesses. Businesses produce all products and services. Businesses create all profits and wealth. Businesses pay all salaries and benefits."[2]

---

[2] Brian Tracy, *Psychology of Selling How to Sell More, Easier, and Faster Than You Ever Thought Possible* (United States: Thomas Nelson Publishers, 2005).

So if our nations businesses were to stop generating sales and started to fail in meeting their daily, weekly, monthly and yearly quotas this would show an early sign of a company's decline, and our economy would go into a recession. Because when people stop buying, businesses stop surviving. So, despite many people expressing their strong disinterest in selling, sales are mandatory for economic growth.

Moreover, by human nature we are all salesmen. Trying to convince me otherwise still requires you to "sell" me on why you're not a salesperson, and the second I buy into your story is the minute your story gets "sold" into my mind. Every day we sell our ideas, opinions and points of view to some of our closest friends, family, co-workers, spouses, acquaintances and peers whether we realize it or not.

Without sales, our success becomes limited. In fact, without sales none of us would get paid, because sales are the bloodline of every business. So how do you ensure you make plenty of sales? By making sure you get customers. How do you get customers? By targeting your market and enticing their impulses through advertising. Trust me, there's a reason why the advertising industry is a $600 billion dollar industry. The purpose of advertising is to keep your business growing and the money flowing.

Every business needs someone who knows how to sell because if sales failed 25 percent of the population wouldn't have iPhones, iPads, iMac's, and so forth. Without sales, the NBA wouldn't generate over $4.5 billion annually, nor would the NFL bring in $8.5 billion, and the numbers continue to climb. So without sales, economies would fail.

THE HEART & SOUL OF BUSINESS

They say sales are the bloodline of any business, but communication will always be the heart and soul of it. This is because communication is a combination of information containing our thoughts, feelings, ideas, and emotions. This information is then expressed, shared and exchanged between two or more people known as the sender and the receiver. The sender is the one who conveys the message whereas the receiver is the one to whom the message was sent.

Therefore, communication is only successful when both the sender and receiver understand the same information contained in the same message. So, as a business owner, when you possess the ability to speak well and know how to convey what you're trying to say to your audience you'll have an advantage when trying to convert potential clients into regular paying customers.

The dynamic principles of communication apply to advertising as well. Because the goal is to leave a lasting impression on your targeted group of customers through television, radio, magazines, newspapers, billboards and internet advertising by skillfully presenting your ideas.

Furthermore, it's because of clear communication that Coca-Cola has managed to sell over 1.8 billion beverages a day since 1997. Once known as the intellectual drink of choice, Coca-Cola is now worth an estimated $56 billion; that's more than Budweiser, Pepsi, Starbucks and Red Bull combined!

Likewise, Louis Vuitton is another great example of how far a clear, solid message can take you and your company, because they dominate the fashion industry. Their consistent message of exquisite luxury tends to draw people in and stimulates them to crack open their wallets and purses to spend. Known for its high-end fashion, Louis Vuitton sells everything from $5,200 petite monogram handbags, to $8,250 briefcases, leather LV emblem trunks, shoes, watches, luggage and other accessories. With their profit margins at almost 40 percent, Louis Vuitton is now worth an estimated $28 billion with over 3,700 locations worldwide.

Moreover, now that we see how clear communication truly is the key to success. We should focus on mastering how to speak and present our ideas in a competent manner in order to boost sales. It's really a matter of choosing the right words in order to accurately convey the right message. Which is why Jim Robin reminds us that "If you just communicate, you can get by, but if you communicate skillfully you can work miracles."

PAY OFF YOUR DEBT

If you're in a lot of debt, like I was, getting out of it may seem impossible, but it's not. The first step is knowing how much you owe and not being afraid to find out. Next, you should formulate what I like to call your "Debt Sheet." On this piece of paper, you will write down your account balances, the organization the account is with, the interest rate, annual APR, and the monthly minimum amount due for each of your debts that are owed. This includes your auto loans, personal loans, payday loans, mortgage, credit cards, and any other reoccurring debts that you may have.

Next, gather all your credit cards. Call each credit card company and ask them for an interest rate reduction; but be ready to negotiate and prepare to play a little hard ball, if necessary. Once complete, update any interest rate changes onto your Debt Sheet. Afterwards, you may want to look into downloading a free app called Debt Payoff Planner (with the bird logo) as it will help provide you with a step-by-step plan that will help you eliminate your debts.

It shows you your payoff summary, the total number of payments left before your balance is paid in full, the total amount of interest you'll accumulate for the life of the loan if you only make the minimum monthly payments, and three different payoff strategies to help you get out of debt faster.

Next, plug in all the info you wrote down on your Debt Sheet into your Debt Payoff Planner and you'll see a concise visual of what you owe and what you may potentially end up paying if you fail to double-up on your payments. After you visually see where you stand financially you should plan how you will reduce your debt by creating a budget and sticking to it. Think of all the ways you can reduce your spending, then calculate your monthly income minus your monthly expenses. Calculate what you'll have left, then decide how much of your remaining income can be put towards your debts. If you work, see if you can put in some overtime, if you're self-employed like me, multiply how many items or services you would need to sell in order to put an extra $1,000 towards your debts each month.

This is a very aggressive approach, so if you can only put an extra $200-$500 towards your debts each month that's ok too. Start with the balance that has the highest interest rate because you'll save on the amount of total interest paid over time. For example, I had a credit card with a balance of $6,084 with an interest rate of 17.5%. If I had kept paying the minimum monthly payments each month it would have taken me 14 years and 11 months to pay it off. So the credit card company would have made $11,010.44 off me in interest alone.

Take note that *interest increases the total amount you owe on the balance due over time*. Most of us are completely unaware of how much this can actually add up to. In total I would have ended up paying back $17,093.44 instead of the original debt of $6,084 if I hadn't decided to pay it off aggressively.

Furthermore, although it is recommended that you pay off the balance that has the highest interest rate, some finance experts advise that if your interest rates across various accounts are around the same APR it would be best from a motivational standpoint to start paying off the accounts with the smallest balance. This approach gives you an influx of determination to keep paying them down until they're finally paid off as you'll feel a sense of victory.

So don't let your debt continue to weigh you down; instead, work hard to pay it down and stick to the debt-free roadmap you created to get out of it.

DIVERSIFYING YOUR PORTFOLIO

You should never invest all your money in one company or product. Instead it's best to diversify your portfolio. Most investment professionals agree that diversification is the most important element of reaching your long-term financial goals as it helps to minimize the risk of losing all your capital in one asset. Although this does not guarantee against loss completely, if done well, diversification can help improve your overall chances of generating a return on your mixed pool of investments.

This practice of spreading your money around has the potential to compliment you financially in the long run. This also helps to prevent you from relying on one single stock choice that may not yield a return. The objective is to protect your stock portfolio from the volatile market by having different investments working simultaneously in your favor. This helps give your portfolio strength even during the worst times in the market. For example, street vendors in New York know that when it's sunny it's easier to sell sunglasses, whereas during the winter months it's easier to sell hats, scarves and gloves.

So, by selling these different items in different seasons they're practicing diversification instead of relying on one single item to keep them in business. Diversification matters because if investment A doesn't work, you still have investments B and C working for you. So by adding different merchandise, more services, or more stores in different markets, you'll have a better chance at generating additional revenue while expanding your company's portfolio successfully.

Diversifying in this way can help your business weather the storm in tough economic times because it provides alternate streams of income in the event that your original market dries up and stops performing, or stops growing, or is hit by new competition. The reasoning behind this technique of diversifying is that a portfolio with different kinds of investments will, on average, yield higher returns and pose a lower risk than any individual investment found within the portfolio.

So remember, when you diversify it makes you less dependent on the performance of one single asset class and helps to give you a higher chance of ensuring a return on your mixed pool of investments.

THE ART OF SELLING

In sales, they say every "no" is one "no" closer to a "yes." Therefore, the art of selling is simply learning how to overcome rejection, while continually striving to make a positive last impression. So when potential buyers refuse to buy what you have for sale, you must keep calm and carry on. Although you may feel like a failure, you're not; it's just that someone failed to buy what you have for sale.

Once you can master breaking through these mental hurdles, these hurdles will no longer break nor master you. It's completely human of you to feel like a loser when you lose a sale. But the most important aspect through it all is to maintain a positive attitude.

See the secret to becoming a serial achiever is becoming a serial believer in your ability to sell. You must also incorporate the art of persuasion into the art of selling if you want to comfortably change a person's mind without them feeling weary. However, this should not be confused with manipulation because persuasion is a formulated system designed by the persuader to convince his or her audience about what he or she is trying to sell, whereas manipulation aims to change the behavior or perception of others through deceptive, dishonest, and sometimes intimidating tactics.

Moreover, persuasion requires you to have strong social skills and an abundant supply of charisma. But sales are not just about being persuasive, they're about having great qualities in your character and reputation. This is what sets salespeople apart, as it establishes a high level of trust. In fact, Warren Buffett said it best, "It takes 20 years to build a reputation and five minutes to ruin it." But what ruins it? Your actions do, because your behavior can disrupt the foundation of trust you worked so hard to establish and leave your reputation in shambles. So think before you act instead of acting before you think. It's no secret that a good reputation keeps generating sales; most importantly it establishes trust. But a bad reputation can cost you millions.

In 2013, Target lost $148 million when they revealed a massive data breach that affected over 40 million of their customers. By 2015 they had finally settled a federal class action lawsuit brought on by customers for $10 million. Target also paid a $67 million dollar lawsuit to Visa, $19 million to MasterCard, and $39 million to several other US banks. Although Target has bounced back and many of their loyal customers have returned, there is still a lesson to be learned about the standard to which a company is held.

Apple, for example, always manages to optimize their brand's reputation, and this helps them to keep generating sales. As a result, they currently have an estimated net worth of $700 billion and are on track to become the first trillion dollar company. Apple is now the biggest and most profitable technology company ever. But they wouldn't be if it weren't for one thing—sales. They have truly made an outstanding masterpiece of how to think differently and push the world forward with new innovative ideas. They have not only established a good reputation but they have also continued to capture the world's attention by always being two years ahead of their time.

This is by far what the art of selling is all about. Paving new roads for your business to grow. Forget what everyone else is doing, focus on what you and your company could be doing—better. The art of selling is about how you communicate, what you communicate, and the way you communicate the relative worth of your brand to the consumer. If you can master these simple insights, then you will without a doubt master the art of selling.

THE ART OF MARKETING

Marketing is simply the process of creating, communicating, and delivering goods and services from concept to the customer. This means the ideas, the brand, the design, sales forecast, market research and the psychology of consumer behavior have all been researched to ensure a successful marketing campaign.

A well thought-out marketing plan will not only help to activate the entrepreneur's venture, but it will also help build on a consumer's impulsive buying behavior and lure them into making a purchase. This is done by skillfully influencing their perceptions and encouraging the consumer to succumb to the temptation of purchasing a product or service because as we all know, perception is everything.

So if I say, "Introducing America's brand new #1 product," and you buy into this statement and regard it as being true (despite the lack of evidence), this belief becomes integrated into your belief system and it may influence your decision to purchase what I'm trying to sell you. In fact, once persuasion and perception become fused in the mind, the mind can no longer distinguish the difference. Every business owner and manager knows this, which is why marketing is such an essential element to the health and survival of any business.

You can bake the best pies in the world but if no one in the world knows about them, you will be the only one eating them. But if you use effective marketing techniques and the right branding tactics, your business can flourish and expand rapidly. This is another reason why marketing is the most critical component in every business. Too often entrepreneurs develop the product but neglect the marketing that pulls the product into the market.

Therefore, your time, energy, money and creativity needs to be allocated towards marketing consistently and consecutively. So decide what you value most about your company, and present it to potential and current customers in a way that displays how it can help benefit them. Figure out what generates more of a response, whether it's an email blast with a headline such as *Buy One Get One Free, Buy One Get One Half Off, or 48 hour 50% off sale*. The more creative you are, the better. Using one of these headlines in the subject line (or one that is similar) in an email blast, or on your social media business page, can help amass a response that may generate more sales.

The objective is to get into the buyer's mind and figure out what works in order to keep people rushing to the checkout line. For instance, I once had a gigantic sign in my clothing store that said, "Can't stop looking at it? BUY IT!" This message alone generated more sales and responses from my customers. But I put that sign up primarily for subconscious reasons, because the subconscious mind stores and retrieves data and does not require you to think, because it's more of a stimulated response that has already been pre-programmed. Best-selling author Brian Tracy couldn't have said it better when he wrote, "Just as your conscious mind can be thought of as the gardener, planting seeds, your subconscious mind can be thought of as the garden, or fertile soil, in which the seeds germinate and grow. Your conscious mind commands and your subconscious mind obeys."

For this reason, marketing to the subconscious mind is vital because on the consumer level emotions affect decisions, and 90 percent of purchasing decisions are made subconsciously. So, as a marketer, you must focus on your product, audience, and most importantly your message because content is everything. The goal should be attract, convert, close, repeat. So for marketing optimization, practice feeding the search engines with your business URL, by indexing your website, your YouTube channel, Facebook fan page, blog and business location on Google, Yahoo and Bing search engines.

This will help your business generate more traffic and can help your content be recognized on the Internet. It will also help you to broaden your reach, your audience and potentially your sales. Furthermore, the art of marketing is not about trying to force people into buying something they don't need. Instead, it's about convincing the consumer that you have the solution to their problem, which is why they need it. So focus on producing a creative marketing campaign that will heighten the consumer's excitement to purchase your product or service. But the main thing that will help your product sell itself is proven results.

Show potential customers how your product is different from anything else out there on the market. Visually distinguish their objections by showing customer testimonials and reviews. This powerful marketing technique can help to infuse new traffic into any business. Also, great reviews on sites like Google, Amazon, and Yelp can help influence people to try your products and services despite a growing list competitors.

What you want your product or service to be known for will shape your entire business. For example, Domino's created the "30-minute guarantee" in 1984, and it helped to make them the world's largest pizza delivery company, with over 5,200 locations. The same can be said about Ford, when they decided to use the tagline, "Built Ford Tough." This helped them heighten the focus on the dependability of their vehicles.

So always think of marketing as spending money to make more money, but you have to get people talking about your products and services in the process. This can be done by encouraging your customers to tell their friends, family and close associates about their experience with your company and how it benefitted them, since that's always what potential clients really want to know—did it work for someone else? Applying these simple strategies can help put you ahead of the competition and possibly keep you there.

THE ART OF BRANDING

The art of branding is simply knowing how to set yourself apart from everyone else. This involves you creatively crafting the image of you, your company, and the product or service you have to offer. Until you, your company and product become a household name. This is why business owners make it their duty to popularize their logo and slogan, because once a company becomes recognized by the general public it strengthens brand awareness and can grow their business tremendously. For this reason, branding will always play an intricate role when aiming to attract new customers.

So how do you actually brand yourself or your company? Well, first you have to define your brand and its attributes, and decide what you or your company want to be known for. What do you want your audience to associate you or your company with when they see and think of you and your brand? For example, when we think of "Coca-Cola," we don't think of pizza, instead we immediately think of a delicious soda in a red can. So in order to build a successful brand you must make sure that people know what to associate it with.

The same can be said when we hear the word "Ferrari." One of the first images that comes to mind is a luxury sports car. But how did Ferrari accomplish this? Simple, by affiliating Ferrari with luxury so that we can associate it with extravagance. They've also managed to create a clever way of keeping their brand of cars exclusive by only manufacturing 7,000 of them per year, which helps it to stay on just about everyone's list of dream cars. So, putting restraints on their production ultimately serves to help preserve Ferrari's value. This clever branding technique influences the consumer's perception that they're getting something rare while this only fuels your desire to drive away with one all the more.

So always keep in mind that your brand is your reputation, and your reputation is based on your past actions and the probability of your future behavior. Apple, for example, has always been known for their Mac PC's, MacBook's, and consumer electronics, such as their iPhones, iPads, and iPods. As a result, their past successes have led to their current success and their current success will most likely lead to their future success.

So if you're pretty adamant about finding your niche market and want your company to succeed, you will have to become an expert in your field. You can achieve this by building a relationship with your potential client base and making sure you deliver what they expect from a reputable company. Because customers want a product or service that is going to respond to their concerns. Branding expert and author Seth Godin says, "A brand is a set of expectations…taken together, for a consumer's decision to choose one product or service over another."

So become a master at demonstrating and explaining why people should buy your product or service instead of your competitor's. Also, focus on building a brand that's cohesive with your company's core values. This helps give your audience an opportunity to recognize your authenticity in the market and will encourage them to believe that you are a brand they can trust.

To expand your brand you will also have to delve into the wonderful world of social media. If you don't have one already, create a Facebook, Twitter, YouTube and Instagram account to help promote and share valuable content about your company's products or services and make it stand out.

Also, refrain from posting things that are inappropriate or offensive and you certainly shouldn't post any of your personal problems on any of your business accounts keep it professional at all times. Focus on strengthening your social network by sparking discussions about your company's products or services to get people talking.

Next, inspire action to gain more traction (i.e. "Subscribe Below," "Like this page," "Learn more," or "Follow me @," on Twitter, Facebook etc.). Also, make sure to include links that will help lead people to your blogs, YouTube Channel, and website. You can share these links in your posts and in the "About" section of your social media account. This way customers know where, when, and how to find you.

Overall, branding is about turning the ordinary into the extraordinary. Today, Twitter has over 300 million active followers, Facebook and YouTube both have over 1 billion monthly users, and Instagram has over 150 million monthly subscribers, and the numbers keep climbing. So I don't see why you or anyone else can't become the next big thing!

THE WORLD IS FULL OF TALENTED POOR PEOPLE

I've always believed that we are who we are because of what we are destined for. You are the only one who can do the things you do, in the unique way that you do them in. Everything from the way you think, to how you behave, to how you go about solving problems, are all a part of your distinct personality. There will never be another you in history, so why not make history?

J.K. Rowling, creator of the Harry Potter fantasy series once said, "I would like to be remembered as someone who did the best she could with the talent she had." I couldn't agree more because it's your talent that propels you into your destiny, so why not let your destiny push you to use your talent?

The Art of Believing & Achieving

Motivational speaker Les Brown, knows that *"One of the richest places on earth is the graveyard. It is there that you will discover people from all walks of life who had high hopes and aspirations that were never fulfilled. Their dreams were visualized but never materialized. Some of the most profound books were never written, the most heartfelt songs were never sung, inventions that were never invented, and cures that could've cured, are all in the graveyard."*

As a result, their self-doubt made them go another route. Their talents never came to life when they had life. This is why learning to have faith in yourself is so important, because when you doubt the power in your talent, you give power to your doubts. In fact, the fault-finding voice you always hear in your head is actually you. That voice that tells you, "I'm not talented," or "I'm not good enough," are your own thoughts.

Every time you set a new goal in place this voice doesn't want you to get ahead, so it gets into your head. Its job is to talk you out of improving yourself. It's the cancer to your confidence. So if we continue failing at silencing our inner critic, the world will continue to overpopulate with talented poor people who doubt themselves. Talented poor people are people who are afraid to trust in their natural ability to pursue opportunities that can potentially improve their lives and the lives of others.

It must be understood that deep inside the heart of every human being is a talent that, if discovered and mastered, can make the world a better place. You'll never live a day outside of your purpose if you bury yourself in your talent on purpose. Your gift is a natural part of your personality, designed for you and your own personal use. The truth is, the world is filled with people who have natural skills, skills that can create opportunities, skills that people will pay to see, skills that can take them around the world and back, because your talent can take you anywhere. So although the world is rich in talent, it's still full of talented poor people.

Let this serve as a reminder that the only thing standing between you and your goals are the excuses that you keep telling yourself. It's not the lack of having money because your talent can produce money for you. It's not a lack of who you know because your talent will find a way to connect you to who you need to know. This is why we must focus on our unique abilities to live life more abundantly. No one is purposeless because all things begin and end with purpose.

So if a job doesn't involve you using the natural gifts you were born with, then you will most likely never experience what you're capable of. Lastly, there's no such thing as someone having a poor talent. No, they just have poor faith in their talent, which makes them talented poor people. It's important to know the difference

WHAT'S HOLDING YOU BACK?

There's a never-ending battle between fear and courage because we can either fear having courage or have enough courage to not fear. For many people, the word "teleportation" conjures up images from a science fiction movie such as Star Trek or Back to the Future. But what if I told you that these images are slowly moving from the realm of science into the realm of reality?

In 2014, Professor Ronald Hanson from Delft University of Technology said, "If you believe we are nothing more than a collection of atoms strung together in a particular way, then in principle it should be possible to teleport ourselves from one place to another…

[therefore] I would not rule it out because there's no fundamental law of physics preventing it."

Two years later, Microsoft created the world's first holoportation device, which is a virtual teleportation system. Although it's still in its infancy this 3D teleportation system makes it look like you're in the same room as someone else when you're actually somewhere else. It functions using Microsoft's HoloLens, which is a really cool holographic computer and a series of 3D cameras that make holoportation possible.

As Bill Gates and his company continue to create the future, what's preventing you from creating yours? Now is the time to seize opportunities to maximize your success. As human beings we possess the amazing power to improve the quality of our lives with our minds, one thought at a time. So the choices we make today influence the consequences that follow. But these same choices can either hurt or help better our tomorrow.

From eating the right foods, to making sure our doors are locked at night before bed, to the jobs we take, and the investments that we make, choices are all around us. Ask yourself, do you want to control your life or would you rather have life control you? So don't let small excuses hold you back from great opportunities.

Self-made billionaire Elizabeth Holmes didn't make excuses when she started Theranos Inc. at 19 years old. Theranos, a consumer healthcare technology company, is dedicated to revolutionizing how we get our blood tested, and was founded by Holmes after she dropped out of Stanford University. She made a conscious choice to follow her passion and discovered a way to help detect the early onset of an illness in time for therapy to be effective. Highly dedicated to her work, she didn't take one vacation in her 20's, she even put dating on hold, and is extremely committed to her profession.

Today she is currently worth an estimated $4.5 billion all because she refused to make excuses and excelled in making the right choices to improve her overall quality of life and the lives of others. Holmes and her company aim to take over the $75 billion lab test industry, and will continue to grow it by another $125 billion, by developing blood tests that detect hundreds of conditions and diseases from just a few drops of blood taken from the finger instead of using tubes of blood from a vein in the arm.

Holmes embodies the true meaning of achieving by believing. She encapsulates the very message I've been trying to convey throughout this entire book, which is walk in your purpose with passion and drive your desire to take action.

LAZINESS WILL STEAL YOUR DREAMS

Success doesn't come easy and it's certainly doesn't come any faster if you're lazy. If producer Kevin Feige, director and screenwriter Joss Whedon were both lazy when it came to mastering their craft, Marvels *The Avengers* would have never been such a success, grossing over $1.5 billion at the box office. Whedon says, "When you're making a film, you have an obligation to fill the frame with life."

The same can be said about our lives; when we're trying to make something of it, we have an obligation to color in each moment with our purpose. But when we neglect the very thing we were designed to do life has its way with you because you're not living in harmony with your purpose. When you neglect pursuing your dreams you'll feel unfulfilled and detached from your destiny because your spirit knows what you're capable of becoming. When we come into this world we have one primary responsibility and that's to find and connect to the reason for why you exist.

Some of us strive to lose weight, go to college, start a new business, find a career, buy a house, get married, start a family, buy a car, pay off our student loans, and so on. But laziness will rob you of achieving these things. Don't you want to experience what life has in store for you? Then stop putting things on hold and telling yourself, "I'm going to do it tomorrow," when you can do it right now. If you don't want to get off your behind and put in the work it takes to be successful, then I have some terrible news for you my friend; you will fail at this thing called life, and you will fail miserably. Because being lazy doesn't produce anything because it's motionless behavior.

Let's say I have a pumpkin seed in my hand but I never sow the seed into the ground. The result will be me not reaping a pumpkin because of my lack of motivation to plant the seed. You can apply this illustration to so many different facets of life. If you continue to talk about all the things you want to do, but never do them, then you're going to live your life complaining about all the things you should've done when you had the chance to do them.

So don't let a goal remain a goal, get going and turn it into an accomplishment! This is what *The Art of Believing and Achieving* is all about, getting things done with your mind first, then your actions. It's about reprograming your thoughts to believe in the very things you desire to achieve. But most importantly, it's about growing your confidence and going after the things in life that really matter to you. The same way working out and staying fit helps to improve your immune system is the same way staying focused and working towards your dreams improves your chances of achieving them. Even when you don't get the results you want don't get discouraged, get motivated! Direct your attention to the things you desire to accomplish and the results will surely follow.

YOU OWE THE WORLD

We live in a world where self-entitlement runs rampant. Not getting what we want makes us want what we're not getting even more. As a result of this, we begin to feel victimized by life as if there was a black cloud lingering over our heads. When we endure a bad experience, lose a person we love or a possession we value, we begin to ask ourselves "Why me?"

But the truth is that the world doesn't owe us a thing. It doesn't owe us a job, it doesn't owe us an inheritance, it doesn't owe us a house, it doesn't owe us a car, it doesn't owe us a college education, it doesn't owe us success, and it certainly doesn't owe us a winning lottery ticket. Instead, we owe the world! We owe the world our unique talents and abilities. We owe the world the changes we can make to it.

So ask yourself, right now, how can I make a difference by being different? Think about how you can leave your mark because your mark is your energy, and your energy is what's needed in order to make a dent in the universe. What do you want to be known for after you leave this physical atmosphere? What accomplishments do you want to leave behind for people to honor and appreciate?

Imagine, if William Cullen didn't demonstrate the first artificial refrigeration process at the University of Glasgow in 1748. It could have possibly derailed American inventor Oliver Evans' purpose to develop the process further in 1805, which inspired Jacob Perkins to physically construct it in 1834. If it weren't for these great men who contributed their gifts to the world, the refrigerator might not exist as we know it. Perhaps we would still be using ice and snow to cool our food and beverages.

It's evident that many conveniences that we enjoy today like the telephone, television, radio, stove, toothbrush, toothpaste, microwave, vacuum, engine, and so on are the result of many years of work by brilliant innovators who were all dedicated to their craft.

You see, we are all born in debt when we come into the world, because we owe the world our gifts. So despite us taking many inventions for granted, let us not forget how they all have helped make a difference in our world, in some significant way or another, because the inventors of those inventions owed them to us.

CHANGE YOUR ATTITUDE

When you have a bad attitude you're carrying around bad energy mentally. As a result, your behavior becomes strengthened by your thoughts and your thoughts become strengthened by your behavior because they both feast off each other. So, if you're mad at the world, you will act upset with those in the world and those in the world may start getting upset with you.

For instance, if you're always thinking about the life you could've had, this habit can result in life going by without you having anything. So know that as long as you have life, you can still work towards what you can have because it's not too late to have it.

Moreover, people who are always cranky, pessimistic, and negative are people who are always unhappy about life. They blame society and feel that the world owes them something; but the world has never owed me, you or anyone, anything. Understand this our lives are like clay, and each day is a new day, as sculptors, to make something of it, no matter how bad our lives may appear to be. The world isn't going to write us a check for our troubles. So having a positive attitude is one of the most powerful mental weapons a person can have to combat the obstacles of life. After all, a positive attitude causes a chain reaction of positive thoughts, events and outcomes.

So expect the best, but always prepare for the worst, yet always look for the good in spite of the bad because a positive attitude can never make matters worse. When you start thinking of what you want, and begin thinking of ways to get it, nothing will be able to stop you from achieving your goals. Without question, one of the most important factors in determining a person's success is the latitude of their attitude when faced with problems.

Ann Landers said it best, "Expect trouble as an inevitable part of life and when it comes, hold your head high, look it squarely in the eye and say, 'I will be bigger than you. You cannot defeat me." Moreover, I believe many of us would agree with how easy it is to have a great attitude when things are going well. But what about when you're faced with adversity and things start going bad? Can you still smile then? Can you still hold your head high and keep a positive mind? Or will you refuse to maintain good energy and instead make your bed in the pit of negativity?

I understand that there are times that we just don't know what to do, where to go or who to talk to. We question if we made the right decisions or if we made all the wrong choices. As uncertainty and doubt emerge so do our fears and it's at that point our emotional responses will be tested. But if we learn to embody the right attitude, we will escape having the wrong attitude. Learning to keep these unwanted emotions at bay helps us stay in a positive frame of mind 95% of the time.

LIFE IS PRECIOUS

One day, while enroute to donate my car to a public auto auction, I was in a terrible car accident in the middle of a five-lane highway. The driver behind me obviously wasn't paying attention and before you knew it I felt the force of impact of a rear-end collision. Unaware of what was happening, my neck immediately whipped back and forth as I felt a very sharp pain jolt up my spine. Everything happened so fast, yet it was happening so slowly. It was as if time stood still and everything around me was moving at a lethargic pace. Within a fraction of a second, which felt like eternity, I saw all of my hopes and dreams flash by in my mind, as I thought of all the things I didn't get to accomplish. It felt like my time was coming to an end, and for a brief moment I actually thought I was dead.

Then, within an instant, it was almost like someone pressed "Play" on my life again, and everything sped up into real time. As I felt the weight of my head dangle across my chest, I could feel the rhythm of my heart pounding as I laid there breathing heavily; my eyes gradually began to open and I could hear the sound of life. As I gently lifted my head, then opened my eyes, I could see 18-wheelers speeding by while vehicles blew their horns and cars swerved in and out of their lanes.

Through my rear view mirror, I could also see a woman with short, dark hair anxiously approaching my vehicle, not knowing what to expect. As she walked up to my passenger side window she quickly asked, "Oh my gosh, sir, are you ok?" Although I was still quite disoriented from the collision, I realized that I was still alive, and that I was still alive for a reason. In that moment I thought to myself, life is precious, so precious that we must cherish every second and not waste another minute, hour, day, week, month or year doing nothing, because life was given to us to be put to use. Truthfully, no one knows the day or hour they will evacuate their body and exit the earth.

Philosopher Pierre Teilhard de Chardin said, "We are not physical beings having a spiritual experience, we are spiritual beings having a physical experience." So make the most of your time here on this Earth, and make every moment count. Smile in the face of adversity, accept full responsibility for your decisions, and learn how to get back up when life kicks you down. Although there will be times when you feel discouraged, stay encouraged.

Enjoy the time you spend with your loved ones, tell your friends and family how much you love and appreciate them, and always be supportive of your kids; and always encourage them to get acquainted with their purpose in life. Teach them the importance of having a strong mind, and to always surround themselves with positive people. Life is precious therefore we were all preciously made. There's a reason why you take over 20,000 breaths a day, there's a reason why your heart beats 60-100 times per minute, and there's a reason why your brain produces enough energy to power a small light bulb. We were all brought into this outer world to share something out of our inner world.

In fact, the *reason* why you exist will always be attached to your *purpose* for living, because your *purpose* for living is the *reason* why you came alive in the first place. Even the Earth is precious as its purpose is to help develop the growth of humanity. It provides us with food, water, nutrients and minerals. It also supplies us with materials for shelter, energy, land, and a multitude of trees and shrubs that give off oxygen that is required for us to live. So as we see, the Earth is precious and so are you. Now is the time to make up your mind, and commit 100% to your dreams, passion and purpose by taking consistent action and not giving up in the process.

PEACE OVER MONEY

One cool December night I began taking inventory in my clothing store and took note of what I had left in stock. I then proceeded to calculate my projected income, and what my profit would be after paying all of my business expenses. Next, I quickly put together a small marketing budget so that I could run a successful Christmas campaign for the holidays.

Shortly thereafter, I remember taking some time to assess the overall health of my business and its functionality. I couldn't deny the overwhelming desire of wanting to turn my store into a multi-million dollar franchise. I thought to myself, "That's when I'll really be happy."

But I suddenly remembered a profound quote by the late, great Bob Marley, who once said, "If it takes money to be happy, your search for happiness will never end." It was at that moment I realized that while I loved making money, I didn't love what money was trying to make me. In all honesty, during that time in my life money was becoming my god. It was the only thing that kept my attention because it was becoming my addiction.

I felt like the thought of making more money was consuming me. I was basing my worth on something that had very little to do with true, long-term happiness. It was as if something was taking over me; like my ego was big, strong and healthy, but internally I was empty. I realized that I was constantly asking myself, "How can I make more money? And how fast?"

Why? Because money has this amazing ability to change a person's life, and it can make some of our wildest dreams come true. Having money is the only way we can buy lavish homes, cars, clothes, wines, jewelry, private jets, plush yachts, and the power, status and fame to go with it. So the more I thought about money the more I began to feel like a hamster on a wheel trying to get to the money. Or more like a rabbit constantly chasing after a carrot on a stick. Except the carrot was always beyond my reach because it was tied to the stick, and the stick was tied to my back.

To me the carrot symbolized money and success, and the stick symbolized my reality, and in my reality those things were becoming harder and harder to obtain because the price tag to live the "American Dream" continues to rise. I couldn't even sleep at night because I was constantly bombarding myself with the same question, "How can I make more money?"

It was like I had to keep finding a different answer to the same question over, and over, and over again. Until one day I finally gave in and realized that I have to be mentally happy with or without money. After all these years, I eventually learned that the more money a man has, the more money he wants. So I gave up trying to fill this hole in my soul because my desire for money was just making it deeper.

The role money plays in our society is a superior one. With over 38 million U.S. households living paycheck to paycheck it's becoming harder and harder to live the "American Dream." To my surprise, according to the American Psychological Association over 72 percent of Americans reported feeling stressed about money and their finances; and nearly 22 percent of

Americans rated their stress levels from 8-10 on a 10-point scale, with 10 being the most. So money appears to be on just about everyone's mind.

In addition, approximately 26 percent of adults in our nation have no savings set aside for emergencies, while another 36 percent have yet to start putting away money for retirement. In fact, the average American is more than $225,000 in debt, with 74 percent having less than $500 in their savings account; despite two-thirds of them who earn a median income of $41,000 a year puting them well above the federal poverty level.

Moreover, the majority of us will spend most of our lives working to pay off our debts to our debtors. The average credit card debt, according to the U.S. household consumer debt profile, is $15,706; the average mortgage debt is $156,333; and the average student loan debt stands at $37,172 with more than 7 million people unwilling or unable to pay off their student loans. Sadly, only 1 in 5 Americans will manage to pay off all their debts in their lifetime.

Unfortunately, our society was governed this way in order to keep us as slaves financially because doing so ultimately limits our freedom. Unless, you're in debt because you decided to invest into something that has the potential to increase in value over time, such as a house or a business.

Otherwise, you have what's called consumer debt which isn't tied to an item that makes money for you and can be seriously detrimental to your life. Consumer debt is the kind of debt you have from things like cars, shopping, electronics, vacations, restaurants, and so forth. These items tend to go down in value or get used up very quickly, leaving you with a pile of bills and sometimes forcing you to work two jobs just to climb your way out of debt. Regardless of the fact that you may hate your job and would love to quit and maybe start your own business. Nevertheless, your financial freedom is limited.

Author DeForest B. Soaries, Jr. said it best in his book *Dfree: Breaking Free from Financial Slavery,* "When we continue to spend what we don't have, charge what we don't need, and borrow more than we can repay, then we must call the problem what it is: slavery." The truth is, the government has been using money as a form of power in order to control us ever since they created it. Why do you think people are always trying to make more money? Because more money gives you more freedom, and more money and freedom give you more power to be free.

Moreover, as the stock market rises and plunges daily, the growing concern about job stability increases, and the cost of health care, auto repair, food and housing continue to rise. Stress, worry and anxiety are present in the corners of our minds. Think about all the investors who worry daily about their investments because they know there's no such thing as a guaranteed return on an investment. Think of the level of anxiety a stock broker deals with on a daily basis, constantly juggling the probability of trying to determine if a certain commodity, stock or currency is going to go up or down without harming their client's account.

Or what about the small business owner who's constantly stressed, like I was, because they know that in order to keep their doors open, customers happy, employees, electricity, and rent paid, they must stay profitable—all while trying not to lose their inner peace, like I almost did. My point is, stress, worry and anxiety all lurk in the corners of the investor, stockbroker and small business owner's mind because of their fear of losing one thing—their money.

So if having money is such a safety net, how safe are we when we can no longer count on our money for safety? In other words, how peaceful would you be if your money were to run out? Throughout history man has held this belief that the more money and possessions we have the more comfortable and at peace and happier we'll be. When in reality having more money may actually make us unhappy and miserable and can take a toll on our well-being.

You see, the only way to have inner peace over money is by organizing our lives around peace with or without money. Allow me to explain. Most of human behavior is controlled by money our lifestyles, jobs, relationships, foods we eat, our government, the colleges we go to, the number of kids we decide to have, the cars we buy, the clothes we wear, and how much we travel are all affected by money. Why? Because we have given money that much power over our lives.

In America money takes the form of coins, and paper which is actually made of cotton/linen material and we use this as an intermediary instrument to facilitate the sale, purchase or trade of goods between parties. We use this as our currency and we look to our currency to measure our wealth. Therefore, we condition our minds to believe that the more money we accumulate, the **happier we'll be**. But this is so far from the truth because **money can't** buy happiness because happiness is free.

The majority of us spend a great portion of our lives chasing the almighty dollar. But what if we stayed in control of being uncontrolled by it? **I'm not saying**, we should all stop striving to make more money, nor am I saying that **money isn't important**, because it is. But what I am saying, is that true wealth is in your mind, not your wallet. So I encourage us all to stay in control of our desire to make more money before our desire to make more money takes control of us. Because money should not dictate our happiness—we should. At last, peace over money means to reside in an internal state of tranquility that is undisturbed, free of stress, worry, anxiety and fear because stress, worry, anxiety and fear are not suited to dwell in a peaceful state of mind.

THE ART OF BELIEVING & ACHIEVING

I wrote the *Art of Believing & Achieving* with the hopes of providing fresh inspiration to anyone chasing a dream in need of some extra motivation. In 2008, a year after serving almost four years in the military, I got fired from a really cool job that I absolutely loved. I was in total shock that they had terminated my employment and wanted me to depart from the company. I couldn't believe what was happening. But even worse was that I had failed to save a substantial sum of money to fall back on.

Making matters worse was the fact that my rent, car note, insurance, credit card bill, cable and utility bill were all going to be due in just a few short days. As my anxiety began to set in I suddenly realized that throughout the entire time of my employment I was depending on my boss to keep food in my mouth. In other words, I was relying on another man to keep my lights on, my rent paid, food in my fridge, gas in my car, clothes on my back and shoes on my feet; and at any given moment, for any given reason, he had the ability to stop feeding me by simply laying me off or firing me.

For me, this was a wakeup call, because growing up my family never tried to broach the subject of entrepreneurship; they were more supportive of us getting jobs. Not that there is anything wrong with having a job, but having a job has never really fit my personality despite the very few ones I had.

It was during that moment that I could feel my inner ambitions begin to stretch as I began to contemplate the idea of venturing onto a different path because I no longer wanted to depend on an employer to take care of me. In reality, I was allowing the security of a paycheck to keep me from my purpose. So I made a radical decision that night at my kitchen table. I promised myself that I'd never wake up and go to work for another man's dream for 8 hours a day, 40 hours a week, for 2,080 hours a year—ever again—as long as I could help it. Instead, I made a choice to invest in me and put that energy towards my dreams. Little did I know that decision would change my life forever, for the better, because I haven't looked back since.

As a result, my life has been nothing short of amazing. I now have the freedom to travel where I want, when I want, for however long I want, without having to request a leave of absence. I determine how much money I want to make whether it's on a daily, weekly or monthly basis. Even when I have slow months, nothing beats the freedom I have being my own boss and surrounding myself around other entrepreneurs—that feeling is priceless.

I've also had the pleasure of starting several different businesses since I was terminated from corporate employment, and I've learned so much in the process. Some of my business ventures were successful and others weren't. But I never let my failures define me; instead, I allowed them to guide me, and motivate me to keep pushing and to put those experiences behind me. When I took a pledge to become an entrepreneur I took it with my heart and I promised myself that I'd be fearless and take calculated risk with a winning attitude no matter what.

There were also times, while traveling on the road less traveled, that I didn't know where I was, or what I was doing, or the direction I was going in. But I still didn't use this as an excuse to give up, although there have been many times I wanted to, I would simply remind myself that some of the ugliest roads can lead us to some of the most beautiful places.

So I fell in love with the journey. I learned how to strengthen my strengths and get acquainted with my purpose, instead of settling for a job to get acquainted with somebody else's. Because I absolutely cherish being the architect of my own destiny as it grants me the liberty to design a life based on my own morals, principles, and beliefs.

Believe me when I say I am living proof that you can be anything you want to be within the parameters of your natural abilities, as long as you focus and believe in yourself. Even without the support of your closest friends and family, including your own parents. I am an example that you can still be successful when you make your purpose your priority. It's natural to want moral and emotional support from the people around you when you're chasing a dream. But the truth is, people will not always encourage you; in fact, most of them will not encourage you at all. However, it's still possible to do what you want to do and make your dreams come true.

I am living proof that you can live a very rewarding life, full of joy regardless of how many obstacles are thrown in your way. I am living proof that you can still come out on top no matter how many times you may fail, just as long as you don't fail to keep getting up. I am living proof that it's never too late to find your way in life before life has its way with you. You just have to believe that you have the ability to achieve, and once you *draw* this picture in your mind, your *art* shall forever set you free.

www.ingramcontent.com/pod-product-compliance
Lightning Source LLC
Chambersburg PA
CBHW020354170426
43200CB00005B/172